Wildlife!

~not your usual slave tale~

by Ramona King

A SAMUEL FRENCH ACTING EDITION

NEW YORK HOLLYWOOD LONDON TORONTO

SAMUELFRENCH.COM

Copyright © 2011 by Ramona King

ALL RIGHTS RESERVED

CAUTION: Professionals and amateurs are hereby warned that *WILD-LIFE!* is subject to a licensing fee. It is fully protected under the copyright laws of the United States of America, the British Commonwealth, including Canada, and all other countries of the Copyright Union. All rights, including professional, amateur, motion picture, recitation, lecturing, public reading, radio broadcasting, television and the rights of translation into foreign languages are strictly reserved. In its present form the play is dedicated to the reading public only.

The amateur and professional live stage performance rights to *WILD-LIFE!* are controlled exclusively by Samuel French, Inc., and licensing arrangements and performance licenses must be secured well in advance of presentation. PLEASE NOTE that amateur licensing fees are set upon application in accordance with your producing circumstances. When applying for a licensing quotation and a performance license please give us the number of performances intended, dates of production, your seating capacity and admission fee. Licensing fees are payable one week before the opening performance of the play to Samuel French, Inc., at 45 West 25th Street, New York, NY 10010.

Licensing fee of the required amount must be paid whether the play is presented for charity or gain and whether or not admission is charged.

Professional/Stock licensing fees quoted upon application to Samuel French, Inc.

For all other rights than those stipulated above, apply to: Samuel French, Inc., 45 West 25th Street, New York, NY 10010.

Particular emphasis is laid on the question of amateur or professional readings, permission and terms for which must be secured in writing from Samuel French, Inc.

Copying from this book in whole or in part is strictly forbidden by law, and the right of performance is not transferable.

Whenever the play is produced the following notice must appear on all programs, printing and advertising for the play: "Produced by special arrangement with Samuel French, Inc."

Due authorship credit must be given on all programs, printing and advertising for the play.

ISBN 978-0-573-69945-0   Printed in U.S.A.   #25738

> No one shall commit or authorize any act or omission by which the copyright of, or the right to copyright, this play may be impaired.

> No one shall make any changes in this play for the purpose of production.

> Publication of this play does not imply availability for performance. Both amateurs and professionals considering a production are strongly advised in their own interests to apply to Samuel French, Inc., for written permission before starting rehearsals, advertising, or booking a theatre.

> No part of this book may be reproduced, stored in a retrieval system, or transmitted in any form, by any means, now known or yet to be invented, including mechanical, electronic, photocopying, recording, videotaping, or otherwise, without the prior written permission of the publisher.

MUSIC USE NOTE

Licensees are solely responsible for obtaining formal written permission from copyright owners to use copyrighted music in the performance of this play and are strongly cautioned to do so. If no such permission is obtained by the licensee, then the licensee must use only original music that the licensee owns and controls. Licensees are solely responsible and liable for all music clearances and shall indemnify the copyright owners of the play and their licensing agent, Samuel French, Inc., against any costs, expenses, losses and liabilities arising from the use of music by licensees.

IMPORTANT BILLING AND CREDIT REQUIREMENTS

All producers of *WILDLIFE!* *must* give credit to the Author of the Play in all programs distributed in connection with performances of the Play, and in all instances in which the title of the Play appears for the purposes of advertising, publicizing or otherwise exploiting the Play and/or a production. The name of the Author *must* appear on a separate line on which no other name appears, immediately following the title and *must* appear in size of type not less than fifty percent of the size of the title type.

CHARACTERS

SAVANNA - Horse healer. Woman who loves horses. Formerly rescued by Honey and Dinah; was a horse stable worker at mansion. Consider: a raspy voice. (African American)

HONEY - Former carnival dancer. Works as a dancer/entertainer on plantation, voluptuous, protective. (African American beauty, brown-to dark skin)

DINAH - Former carnival dancer. Works as a dancer/singer, was (non-sexual) entertainment for parlor, sassy young sister of Honey. (African American - light skin)

MRS. ANAZET - Kidnapped plantation missus, married to Mister. Shrewd business woman, well-to-do. Heritage: questionable. White and looks it, but is rumored to be a black woman. Cast as white/fair skin palette, may be blond or red hair. (White - fair skin)

SINGING RAIN, a.k.a. **RAIN** - Fugitive. Was married to Bullet's brother John, now deceased. Unstable health. Native American mother of Conchata. Haunted, wants safety for her daughter.

BULLET - Fugitive wanted for escape and assisting in escape of others. Money on her head. Sister-in-law to Singing Rain (John's sister). Heritage: African-American, predominantly African.

CONCHATA - Fugitive. Nine year old daughter of Rain. Wisdom gatherer. Occasionally walks with a slight limp. Heritage: Afro-Native American.

ADULT CONCHATA - Confident, beautiful, wealthy, regal, has kept her culture elegantly.

CHARLOTTE - Ghost child. Five or six years old, petite. Honey's missing daughter. White - fair skin color. Contrast in skin color to **HONEY**.

MAN IN BOOTS/WALKING BOOTS

OTHER FIGURES

MYZION - Stunningly beautiful, intelligent, fine, black male horse. (Offstage, unless producers have the wherewithal for a walkthrough at end of the play)

JUDAH - Brown-black, Intelligent horse (but they all are).

THE TREE - Thick full feminine. Branches everywhere, alive, listening, protective. Spiritual.

ALL THE LIVING - Morning sun. Night. Moon. Creatures. Fiona and flowers.

None of the above women (or horses) are currently enslaved. They wouldn't have it.

SETTING

Deep in the wooded forest.

TIME

1800s prior to Civil War.
Mysterious autumn.

AUTHOR'S NOTES

Where noted, skin color is vitally important to character and believability. Therefore the author strongly directs that certain roles be cast accordingly.

The role of **ANAZET** is strongly directed to be cast with a white woman or European woman and not someone who could possiblably "pass." If there is a hint that **ANAZET** could be of African heritage the believability is defeated and so is the central life/death tension of *WILDLIFE!*

DINAH is suggested to be light skin. **HONEY** is darker than Dinah; consider all brown skin color palettes. There can be great skin color contrast between the sisters as often is the case in Afro American families.

BULLET is the oldest, the wisest and not perfect, not sexless. Her frame is solid–be she thin or heavy set–but like the rest...she can handle it.

SINGING RAIN is second to the oldest. The spirit of the actor dictates the age because she can have a baby at the age/s she wants.

SAVANNA is not light skinned. She looks like she could have been born on a horse – agile, somewhat quiet.

CHARLOTTE is a mixture. White-very fair skin, nearly blond. Her looks tell the story.

ADULT CONCHATA (20's). She appears, with the presence of clarity, strength, wealth, and intelligence. She is not old looking. Attractive, inside and out. She walks with her-story.

The women are agile as if their lives depend on it...and it does.

THE AMBUSH SCENE

The ambush/death scene is performed in slow motion in dark shadowy lighting. It is directed that the bodies are covered and to the side of the stage–out of the way–so that the following scenes do not have distraction. The bodies are lined together on the floor and slightly hidden (waist to head) from the audience by overturned furniture without appearing disrespectful. Strongly directed: in total black out actors move to the side, lie on floor and half cover their bodies. If there cannot be total black out–have darkest lighting. Actors move slow motion to the side, lay on floor, half cover themselves. Position actors so that audience is not distracted.

Dinah's little flower: in the ambush scene the jar/vase of Dinah's little flower to Conchata is stabilized so that it remains intact. Often there is one thing that remains intact through chaos–the flower in the jar is that thing.

Costumes and hair have multiple ways to style especially secret pockets and hidden places in the fabric. All the women are prepared even to hide a flower. Sleeves, ties, ribbons, dress length may all be played with. Maintaining distinction between wild and unkempt.

Be Brave...and have a great ride.

Flight 2010,
For my first Love:
Margo Marie Kyzer King,
The grace, the courage, wisdom & laughter,
My jazzy mom.

PROLOGUE I

(Absolute blackness.)

(Voice offstage or recorded)

CONCHATA. Once, long ago, where I lived in the midst of the woods, under the blue pines, near the rivers, when I had soft walking bones, I had seven mothers, seven wonder-filled mothers, in the midst of the woods, who gave me who I am.

PROLOGUE II

(Seven spirits. Women in dark silhouettes, semi-circle around **CONCHATA** *in various levels of prayer positions. Sound of horses whinnying throughout the whispering prayers. Each prayer is picked up by the next line as if this is one spoken prayer. Music plays [suggested music: Franz Schubert: Ave Maria/instrumental or suspenseful/classical music] very softly beneath prayer.)*

(They join in a recitation of Psalms 16)

DINAH. *(Psalm 16:5)* The Lord is the portion of mine inheritance and of my cup: thou maintainest my lot.

ANAZET. *(Psalm 16:6)* The lines are fallen unto me in pleasant places: yea. I have a goodly heritage.

HONEY. *(Psalm 16:7)* I will bless the Lord who hath given me counsel: my reins also instruct me in the night season.

SINGING RAIN. *(Psalm 16:8)* I have set the Lord always before me: because he is at my right hand. I shall not be moved.

BULLET. *(Psalm 16:9)* Therefore my heart is glad, and my glory rejoiceth: my flesh also shall rest in hope.

SAVANNA. *(Psalm 16:10)* For thou will not leave my soul in Hell; neither will thou suffer thy holy one to see corruption.

(The lights begin to fade - remaining on **CONCHATA.***)*

CONCHATA. *(Pslam 16:11)* Thou will show me the path of life: in thy presence is fullness of joy: at thy right hand there are pleasures forever more. Thou will show me the path of life: in thy presence is fullness of joy...

(fade to black)

ACT I

Scene One

(Except for sketches of the moon entering the paper-thin tiny shack/shelter, total blackness. Night sounds, creatures, movement wind and trees. Branches snapping. Sudden sound of thin wooden door violently busted wide open. Quick footsteps, panicked breathing, a hand covering a screaming muffled voice, sound of dragging a kicking body. The muffled voice and body struggle and continue into dialogue until exit. The women speak in hushed, panicked, staccato voices.)

(Myzion and Judah make loud whinnying warnings throughout scene. The door bust open. Dialogue is wild and rapid.)

DINAH. *(edging hysteria)* I ain't did it – I ain't did it – they gon' think I did it–

(hushed panic)

HONEY. SAVANNA!!!   **SAVANNA.** *(scared)* AHHH!!!

(SAVANNA is violently fighting. Overlapping clear dialogue.)

SAVANNA. *(loud and fighting)*   **HONEY.** *(hushed)*
Get away! Take your   It's me Honey! Honey!!
hands off me!
Git your hands off me!!!

*(**HONEY** violently shakes her to calm her down.)*

SAVANNA. *(toning down confused)* Honey? What you doin'?

HONEY. *(rapidly spoken)*   **DINAH.**
  Hush up damnit!   I ain't did it, I ain't-

(HONEY begins pushing SAVANNA out of bed.)

HONEY. *(to SAVANNA)*   **SAVANNA.**
  SAVANNA COME ON!   HUH?! WHAT?!
  COME ON! WE
  GOTTA LEAVE!

(The sound of HONEY pulling SAVANNA to her feet.)

HONEY. Git up Savanna! Git up!

SAVANNA. Huh? Where we goin'?

HONEY. GIT UP!

SAVANNA. Where to?

HONEY. Mizta dead. Blood everywhere. We got trouble.

(silence)

DINAH. *(as to wake her)* We in trouble!!!

SAVANNA. *(rapid dialogue as Savanna pulls on boots and moves)* Ah! You'll go!

HONEY. *(Not a question)* You comin!

SAVANNA. Take MyZion and Judah.

DINAH. NO! Don't separate.

DINAH. *(chants)*   **HONEY.**
  Keep together, keep   -Where? Where we goin'?
  together!

SAVANNA.
  Follow MyZion,
  ride East
  Near the river, be a   **HONEY.** *(repeats fast)*
  'lil shack   East, waters, shack
  under blue pines   **DINAH.**
    I didn't do it. I didn't do it.

HONEY.	**DINAH.**
We goin' to that woman?	Don't separate, don't!

SAVANNA. Ride near the waters, MyZion knows…

(Sound and movement of **HONEY** *backing out with* **DINAH** *and a kicking body.)*

HONEY. *(command)* You be there, Savanna, hear me? Follow us, hear me?!

SAVANNA. Go 'head now! What in hell is that? *(referring to kicking)*

HONEY. *(command)* Come Dinah!

DINAH.	**SAVANNA.**
Come wit us. Come wit us. We can't leave her!	Go on now!

(Sound: Inaudible whispers continue, muffled screams, quick footsteps, horses snorting, riding off into full gallop sounds begin to overlap then fade into the following scene.)

Scene Two

(Thin shack/shelter.)

(A bare shelter, less than a shelter. The home has been built around a tree growing through it. Crude and amazing. Hard-edge fairy tale looking but no mistaking the almost borderless blur between home and earth around it. There is a trap door underfoot. Two straw stuffed beds-created with bark, vine and nature scraps, raw beautiful blankets, a tin basin sculpted by a storm, elaborately shaped water buckets, yellowing curled posters. Dwelling neat, clean, minimal. Nature adores it, especially the tree.)

*(A stand-off in process: **SINGING RAIN** and **BULLET**. **BULLET** on one side of the shelter, **SINGING RAIN** on the other. **SINGING RAIN** is sick and physically strong.)*

SINGING RAIN. Where? You tell me now! Now!

*(**SINGING RAIN** runs about the shelter searching, knocking things over.)*

Tell me! Why don't you tell me where?

BULLET. *(trying to calm her)* That's all right sister, gon' be all right.

*(**SINGING RAIN** drops down to the floor and begins scratching and digging as if it were earth.)*

SINGING RAIN. Here? I know, I know. No. Here!

BULLET. Come on and stop it. It's all right…

SINGING RAIN. Help me, help me!

*(**SINGING RAIN** pantomimes taking the rope off the neck of her husband John, who hangs from a tree. Abruptly, **SINGING RAIN** stops.)*

(She runs, scattering the shelter.) You want to take her? *(She pantomimes clutching a new baby.)* Where is my baby?! *(Suddenly, she opens her empty arms.)* They take her?! Did they take her?! You take her to the mountains? Where is my baby? Did they take her from me?!

(There is knocking sounds underfoot. **BULLET** *returns the sound, stomping a quick signal. Knocking stops.)*

SINGING RAIN. *(again, she continues to wild-scatter the shelter:)* Take it down. I can't see him, I can't see him! Take your skirt down!!! *(She relives* **BULLET** *holding her skirt wide to block the sight)* John, where? JOHN!!! Find the baby! The horses, grab her, the horses! *(to* **BULLET***)* Help me, help me! *(Again, she drops and scratches the earth.)*

BULLET. *(trying to calm her)* I'm here.

SINGING RAIN. Cover her! Cover her eyes!

BULLET. I have her. Conchata can't see a thing.

*(***SINGING RAIN*** pantomimes again, taking John from the tree and removing the rope.)*

SINGING RAIN. *(She holds out her arms for her baby.)* John, I'm here, I'm here. I come soon with you…soon with you…Where's my baby? Soon with you John, I stay here, I can't leave now. No, no…

BULLET. We're here now. We safe. Look 'round. John chase 'em off.

*(***BULLET*** attempts to hold and comfort her. The two women begin to struggle.)*

I'm here wit ya, my sister. They gon' see…Look, John chase 'em.

*(***SINGING RAIN*** slowly begins to sink, murmuring as she calms. She is heaving, physically worn.* **BULLET** *leads her to bed. She lays down and travels in a trance.)*

SINGING RAIN. *(softly)* Can't see him…can't see him…

BULLET. Stay with me, sister. *(speaking to spirit John)* Don't come for her just yet, John. Help us first 'cross them waters. I can't run 'lone no 'mo. 'Chata needs her momma.

*(***SINGING RAIN*** begins to cough.* **BULLET** *walks to the water buckets, wets a cloth, puts it to* **SINGING RAIN***'s face.)*

(**BULLET** *returns to the bucket, dips the cup in but freezes, urgently listening. Suddenly, as if she is lightening: drops cup, dims lights, grabs hidden rifle. Crisp swift moves.*)

(*Sound/night black: Footsteps of humans and snorting horses.* **HONEY**, **DINAH**, *and* **ANAZET**: *exterior of shelter. Sound of horses and humans walking and then coming to a halt.*)

(*The women are exhausted, afraid, dangerous.*)

DINAH. (*out of breath*) Where are we? This be it?

HONEY. Looks like.

DINAH. Who inside?

HONEY. I'm out here wit you.

DINAH. (*rapid*) What you see?

HONEY. Same thing you do.

DINAH. What?

HONEY. Nothin'.

DINAH. Maybe we wrong. Maybe we should wait for Savanna, we should–

HONEY. Hush up!

DINAH. I.…I didn't do it, Honey.

HONEY. You weepin'?

DINAH. (*half-weeping*) No, I ain't weepin'!

HONEY. Keep ya eyes loud open. We ain't safe. What you say?

DINAH. I'm beside ya. I'm behind ya, all around ya.

HONEY/DINAH. I'm wit ya.

HONEY. We got to git out the open. Crawl up there, when I tell ya, look round first, here, throw these here stones near that door. 1, 2…4! Go!

DINAH. It's 1, 2, and 3.

HONEY. Ain't I said that?

DINAH. No.

HONEY. Yes, I did.

DINAH. No, you didn't!

HONEY. Yes, I did!

DINAH. Listen, 1, 2, 3, like that. Like 1, 2, 3, 4, 5, 7, 9, 17. That's counting.

HONEY. Ain't any 7, 9, 17.

DINAH. Oh yeah...

HONEY. Who told ya that? Never mind. Just git up there. I got the horses, cover for ya. Crawl soft, here throw this...Anazet, you keep playing dead or you won't have to.

DINAH. ...and if it's men..?

(silence)

HONEY. Ya come high tail back here. Ya hear me? Won't be no men. Savanna knows.

DINAH. I throw these here stones–

HONEY. 'till she opens up...tell her ya got your sista here and need shelter for the night.

DINAH. How ya know it's her?

HONEY. Tell her, Dinah! Don't come back here 'till ya do. I'm right 'hind ya.

DINAH. Ya not right 'hind me, you gon' be way back here.

HONEY. With a loaded gun.

*(Sounds crawling, three stones thrown, lights further dimmed. Door opens slightly. Silence. **BULLET** makes a Yoruba sounding call.)*

BULLET. *(Nearly singing)* Ye-MA-Ya ...Ye-Ma-Ya...

DINAH. *(Nervous and shaky)* Evening' Ma'am.

(silence)

(a very poor, shaky, singing reply) A My My My to ya too Ma'am,

(silence)

BULLET. What the hell...? Show yourself.

*(**BULLET** commands from within the shelter.)*

DINAH. *(nervous)* Ah…Ah, Ma'am, we shelter got need, my brother, my sister, sister for the day night have shelter got you a sister day for now, please Miss Ma'am?

(pause)

BULLET. Who the hell's there?

DINAH. Dinah. Name's Dinah. My sista broke her foot and we need to sit down. We needin' help.

BULLET. *(to herself)* Got crazy womenfolk out here. *(to **DINAH**)* "We" got a number?

DINAH. Ain't but three.

(**DINAH**, **HONEY**, *and* **ANAZET** *appear. Door opens wider.* **BULLET** *appears with rifle. Following interaction is rapid.*)

BULLET. *(commands)* Come up here.

DINAH. *(whispers nervously)* …Honey?

HONEY. *(whispers back)* I'm wit ya.

BULLET. Who ya'll?

HONEY. Name's Honey. This be my baby sis' Dinah.

BULLET. *(pointing to **ANAZET**)* Who's that?

HONEY. Ah…Anazet. She took a fall.

BULLET. What ya'll want?

HONEY. Shelter, we gon' 'fore daybreak.

BULLET. Ya'll runnin'?

(silence)

Just ya'll?

HONEY. My good sista friend comin' after.

BULLET. *(alarmed)* Somebody trackin' ya here? Who?

HONEY. She just colored.

BULLET. Who, I said?!

HONEY. Savanna! Name's Savanna.

BULLET. Them horse I smell?

HONEY. Hitched 'em yonder, best still we tied 'em up close. Can we?

BULLET. *(command)* Come up here.

(**SINGING RAIN** *has come out of the shelter circled behind the women holding a rifle on them.*)

SINGING RAIN. Move!

DINAH. *(whispers to* **HONEY***)* Savanna know her, too?

HONEY. Hush!

(**BULLET** *looks from* **HONEY** *to* **DINAH** *but halts when she gets a close look at* **ANAZET.** **BULLET** *gets into* **ANAZET***'s face, studying her.*)

BULLET. This a white woman?!

(**BULLET** *now notices* **ANAZET***'s hands tied behind her back.*)

SINGING RAIN. *(a statement)* She's white.

DINAH. *(quickly shooting her mouth)* Heifer colored just like us, just light-skinned heifer. She a parasol carryin' nigra.

HONEY.	**DINAH.**
Dinah!	But a colored and nigra just the same.

ANAZET. Yes, I am a white woman.

HONEY. *(to* **ANAZET***)* 'Member what I said.

DINAH. Shut up, Anazet. Ya born colored just like the rest of us. Ya fuzzy yella hussy!

ANAZET. I am telling you right now for your own survival, cut me loose. I'll have you two spared.

BULLET. Spared?!

ANAZET. *(blurting out)* They've kidnapped me! Obviously! *(quickly half-turns to show tied hands)* They've taken me against my will. She murdered-

(**DINAH** *interrupts* **ANAZET** *with a hook to the jaw, knocks her to the floor.*)

BULLET. What's goin' on here?

SINGING RAIN. She's white, they follow.

ANAZET. That's right they're coming to collect me. You better damn well let me go before they kill you! Kill you for taking me against my will!

DINAH. Shut ya nigra mouth! 'Cause a you we runnin'!

HONEY. Dinah!

BULLET. Back out!

HONEY.	**DINAH.** *(indignant)*
Huh?	What?!

(Following dialogue is spoken: excited rapid clear articulated.)

BULLET. Keep ridin'.

SINGING RAIN. Leave the horses.

BULLET.	**HONEY.**
Ya ain't stayin'.	Our horses?!

SINGING RAIN. Give us one horse.

HONEY.	**SINGING RAIN.** *(to BULLET)*
It ain't like ya thinkin', please!	Take Conchata, ride now.

BULLET. BACK OUT! *(referring to ANAZET)* And take her wit ya!

ANAZET. Cut me loose!

DINAH. I told y'all she's ain't white. She 100% Nigra.

HONEY. Ain't no place to turn.

(The following is spoken simultaneously twice:)

ANAZET. Cut me loose!	**BULLET.** Can't chance it! Back out!
HONEY. We ain't goin'	
DINAH. Damnit! I said she's lying!	**SINGING RAIN.** We take horses!

*(**ANAZET** manages to get back on her feet and makes a run for the door. **HONEY** throws **ANAZET** into **SINGING RAIN** and **BULLET**.)*

HONEY. *(to* **DINAH***)* Dinah! Now!

> (**HONEY** *and* **DINAH** *rush* **SINGING RAIN** *and* **BULLET**. *Quickly, but breifly, they struggle with guns and rifles with* **ANAZET** *in between them, until they overcome the two.)*

HONEY. We ain't leaving!

DINAH. Get down! Now, ya'll shut up!!!

> (**DINAH** *looks at* **ANAZET** *who is silent.* **DINAH** *whacks* **ANAZET** *to the floor.)*

DINAH. *(to* **ANAZET***)* I said, shut up!

HONEY. *(to* **BULLET** *and* **SINGING RAIN***)* On them knees.

> (**BULLET**, **SINGING RAIN**, *and* **ANAZET** *stand on their knees.)*

DINAH. *(to* **ANAZET***)* I said, on them knees!

HONEY. *(to* **DINAH***)* She is.

DINAH. Oh.

> (**HONEY** *and* **DINAH** *circle the women checking around the shelter as they speak.)*

HONEY. Savanna said ya gon' help me and my sista and ya gon' do it!

DINAH. What we do now?

HONEY. Git the horses up close.

> *(There is knocking underfoot.* **HONEY** *and* **DINAH** *look around.)*

HONEY. What's that?

DINAH. What?

HONEY. Hush.

> (**BULLET** *and* **SINGING RAIN** *slightly look at one another as if in signal.)*
>
> *(silence)*
>
> *(Again, there is knocking underfoot.)*

DINAH. Come from here.

HONEY. *(to BULLET and SINGING RAIN)* What's that? *(as if she knows that they know)*

(silence as HONEY eyes BULLET and SINGING RAIN)

HONEY. *(to DINAH)* Go over there.

(DINAH walks near the area of the hidden trap door. SINGING RAIN and BULLET clearly tense up as HONEY continues to eye them. DINAH rocks her foot back and forth to the indentation on the floor. She kicks back the blanket covering it.)

DINAH. *(childlike amazed)* Look, it's a lil' door.

HONEY. *(Serious, to SINGING RAIN and BULLET)* What's in there?

(DINAH taps her foot around the door and the door begins to open slightly. DINAH jumps back. SINGING RAIN runs to the door, slams her foot defiantly down on it.)

SINGING RAIN. You kill me first.

DINAH. Hot damn and shit, too! What the Hell..? Somethin' breathing in there?

BULLET. *(to SINGING RAIN. BULLET rises and stands by RAIN's side)* Open it.

DINAH. *(to BULLET and SINGING RAIN)* Get down…or something…

(HONEY and DINAH are confused. SINGING RAIN taps her foot in code then moves her foot. The door slowly opens. SINGING RAIN helps CONCHATA out. HONEY, upon seeing CONCHATA appear out of the trap door forgets everything and goes into a trance. CONCHATA has a gun, which she promptly hands to her mother. CONCHATA stands between BULLET and RAIN peeking out amazed at the company. RAIN aims the gun at HONEY and DINAH.)

HONEY. *(to CONCHATA)* CHARLOTTE! Oh Lord, it's Charlotte.

DINAH. *(speaks very gently)* My sista, that ain't Charlotte.

(**HONEY** *puts her gun down and falls to her knees looking at* **CONCHATA**.)

DINAH. *(to* **BULLET** *and* **RAIN***)* My sista, she gits confused.
HONEY. Charlotte…
DINAH. She won't hurt her none.
BULLET. *(quietly)* Ease them guns over.
SINGING RAIN. *(quietly)* Now.

(**DINAH** *reluctantly slides the guns to* **BULLET**. **HONEY** *is oblivious, focused only on* **CONCHATA**. *Quietly and slowly* **ANAZET** *comes to her feet.*)

HONEY. You thought she was gone…My Charlotte. It's been so long, but a mother can't forget. Come here, baby.

(**HONEY** *opens her arms wide.*)

Please. Please come, darlin'.

DINAH. *(to* **SINGING RAIN** *and* **BULLET***)* She won't hurt her none.

HONEY. Ya recognize me, don't ya?

(**CONCHATA** *looks to her mother.* **RAIN** *nods, cocks gun aiming it low at* **HONEY**. *Slowly* **CONCHATA** *walks over to* **HONEY**.)

HONEY. You grown so and you pretty, too. May I hug ya, darlin'? Let momma hug ya, let momma finally hold ya again. You remember me, my lil Love? My lil Love.

(**CONCHATA** *turns to her mother* **SINGING RAIN** *slowly nods.* **HONEY** *hugs the air. She does not touch* **CONCHATA**.)

HONEY. My baby. I always been lookin' for ya. My baby girl. I know its alla sudden for ya, but I been so waiting. Been waiting a hundred forevers. I just knew…always tellin' ya Aunt Dinah, you gon' come one day…You gon' come…You gon' come back to me. I don't even have nothing' for ya.

(**DINAH** *is sad, bit embarrassed, defeated. The women strongly understand situation as they continue to aim the guns low.*)

DINAH. *(to* **BULLET** *and* **SINGING RAIN**) She ain't gon' 'member none after.

HONEY. Here, let me give ya something.

(She looks around and then on herself. There is nothing. She reaches up to her head and tears a piece of her hair out, ties it in a knot.)

HONEY. Next time I'll have somethin' for ya, darlin'.

(She hands the hair to **CONCHATA**. **CONCHATA** *reaches for the imaginary hair. Suddenly* **HONEY** *looks around.* **CONCHATA** *remains standing in front of* **HONEY**.*)*

HONEY. *(wild and frantic)* Charlotte! Charlotte! Where she go? Where's Charlotte? Dinah, where's Charlotte?

(As this scene plays **ANAZET** *has slowly been making her way to the door.* **BULLET** *stops her with the gun.)*

BULLET. *(to* **ANAZET**) No.

*(***DINAH** *notices and runs for* **ANAZET**. **HONEY** *snaps back.* **CONCHATA** *runs back to her mother.)*

HOLD IT!

DINAH. *(to* **ANAZET**) First chance. I'm gon' git ya like "I" own ya.

BULLET. Now ya'll git on the floor.

(The women obey. But **BULLET** *freezes as she listens to the outside.* **SINGING RAIN** *picks up and listens too until all the women are frozen, listening.* **SINGING RAIN** *dims the lights. Sound: horses snorting and walking.)*

HONEY. *(whispers)* It's Savanna.

BULLET. *(whispers)* How ya know it ain't someone followed ya here?

HONEY. It's her.

BULLET. Git up, call to her.

*(***BULLET** *opens the door.* **HONEY** *steps into the door.)*

SAVANNA. *(hushed low voice, searching)* Ye-Ma-Ya…Ye-Ma-Ya… Honey? Miss Bullet?

HONEY. Savanna... Savanna.

SINGING RAIN. *(to BULLET)* She know your name.

SAVANNA.	**BULLET.**
Honey?	...and my call...

HONEY. *(to BULLET)* What ya want me to tell her?

BULLET. Hold her fire up.

HONEY. Savanna, guns up.

> *(SAVANNA walks up to the shelter, guns high. SINGING RAIN brings the lights up. SAVANNA enters. She notices DINAH and ANAZET on their knees.)*

BULLET. *(to SAVANNA)* Drop.

> *(SAVANNA looks at HONEY. HONEY nods. SAVANNA kneels. Dialogue rapid. Door slightly open, RAIN searches the outsides with her eyes remaining in shelter.)*

BULLET. *(a threat in command)* How ya know my name? How ya know my call?

SAVANNA.	**BULLET.**
I...I...	How ya find me? They nail my face to trees?

HONEY. Tell her!

BULLET. Ya huntin' for 'em?

SAVANNA. Hunt?! No Ma'am.

BULLET. *(not a question)* They sent ya huntin' for me?

SAVANNA. No!

DINAH. Shit no!

SAVANNA. Met ya–

BULLET. *(sizing her, testing her)* –Ya ain't met me!

SAVANNA. Sometime back.

BULLET. Where?!

SAVANNA. *(nervous, confused)* Was, was you–

BULLET. -Was not! I can 'call faces! Who follow ya here?!

SAVANNA. -Ain't nobody-

BULLET. -Huh?!

SAVANNA. *(speaks rapidly)* Was you, box car, this here woman, a child, 'lil baby, a man…

  (**BULLET** and **SINGING RAIN** *look at one another.*)

  (pause and then pause again)

BULLET. *(quiet-careful)* How ya know this?

SAVANNA. *(rapidly but clearly spoken)* Ya secret to some but I–

BULLET. I give ya three more breaths to tell it.

SAVANNA. …Thomasville! –Was in Thomasville. When I show horses to yonder counties, talk be 'bout ya.

BULLET. Ya got one breath left.

SAVANNA. We ain't no hunters, ya can plain see that, but I ain't gon' lie, we left trouble.

BULLET. And dropped it here.

SINGING RAIN. They comin' for her. *(pointing to ANAZET)*

SAVANNA. I covered the tracks. Rest horses, find direction, we gone.

SINGING RAIN. *(suddenly fast and curious)* Where?

BULLET. *(reads SINGING RAIN)* No!

SAVANNA. I'm hoping Miss Bullet tell us.

BULLET. I don't no more take folk 'cross.

DINAH. *(dumbfounded)* What she say?!

SAVANNA. Ya tell me, I can follow most any path–

HONEY.	**DINAH.**
–she can.	She found you.

SAVANNA. –Just don't know what to take.

BULLET. I ain't who I was.

HONEY. *(To SAVANNA)* This be the woman?

SAVANNA. We can't git caught.

BULLET.	**SINGING RAIN.** *(softly)*
I don't no more take folk 'cross, now that's flat.	They got horses.

HONEY. *(surprised)* This be her?

SAVANNA. *(to* **BULLET***)* Ya mean, not now…?

BULLET. Not ever.

HONEY. Not ever..?

DINAH. What kinda rabbit shit is this?

SAVANNA. *(slightly confused)* Ya got direction, don't ya?

DINAH. Don't ya?!

BULLET. Just gave it.

DINAH. Ya ain't gave a mule's behind!

HONEY. Savanna, now–

DINAH. She gotta tell us! We gotta git, damnit!

SAVANNA. *(confused)* Ain't never been this far yonder.

HONEY. *(to* **SAVANNA***)* She know, don't she?

DINAH. Well, don't she?!

SAVANNA. *(to* **BULLET***)* 'Gon' be word on us. Horses weak, no stars. Gon' come morning.

DINAH. MORNING?!

SAVANNA. We needin' ya help.

DINAH. MORNING?! Ya must got wind in them ears!

HONEY. We be leavin' sooner, ain't we?

DINAH. Four black behinds, one behind pretendin' it ain't, best be sooner flying over them hills way 'fore daybreak–

SAVANNA.	**DINAH.**
Miss Bullet–	–way 'fore daybreak, Savanna!

DINAH. *(to* **BULLET***)* Now open that damn blasted "Ye-Ma-Yo yappin'" trap o' yours and spill it, damn it! We gotta git!

SAVANNA. We needin' help, Miss Bullet–

BULLET. *(unhelpful, very)* Don't we all.

ANAZET. –Cut me loose and you won't have need for–

DINAH. –Too late. Dead or blinkin' them gon' want ya pink behind. What ya think they gon' do to a colored woman trickin' 'em? Master's brother ain't gon' like that. They gon' flame ya piggy pink butt up. They gon' flame ya back to your natural black!

ANAZET. Nasty, low mouth, nigra wenches. Spreading lies like disease. Miss Bullet, Miss Indian, I won't allow any harm to come to you, release me! I'll see to it that–

(DINAH interrupts her with that hook. ANAZET doubles over grasping for breath. Ignored.)

DINAH. –Look 'round, this look like ya big house?

SAVANNA. We'll keep out ya way.

SINGING RAIN. You fight, you go.

BULLET. *(to SINGING RAIN)* What? Ya don't gon' soft for sure! They ain't stayin'.

SINGING RAIN. *(points to head)* And ya done gon' empty!

BULLET. Look who talkin'.

SINGING RAIN. They got horses!

BULLET. They can't help us.

SINGING RAIN. They got horses–wind head.

BULLET. They know we're here. Who else gon' know?

SAVANNA. We covered the–

SINGING RAIN. Stay!

(silence)

SINGING RAIN. *(to BULLET)* Tell 'em 'bout the river.

SAVANNA/HONEY. What river?

BULLET. *(back at SINGING RAIN)* You tell 'em!

SINGING RAIN. I don't know river like you.

BULLET. That's just too bad.

(Silence at that. SAVANNA looks slowly over to BULLET who is steaming. Pause.)

DINAH. *(panicked)* That's it? She ain't said shit, we don't know shit, now we ain't got shit.

(pause)

SINGING RAIN. *(sarcastic)* We got water…and food.

SAVANNA. Thanks Miss–

DINAH. *(as in help)* Honey..?

(HONEY reading the situation, motions DINAH to stay calm.)

SINGING RAIN. Singing Rain. Call me, Rain.

SAVANNA. Thanks.   **HONEY.** *(whispering to* **SAVANNA***)* What we gon' do now?

SAVANNA. *(whispering to* **HONEY***)* Gotta talk to her.

DINAH. Talk! I say we break now. I say four behinds fly over 'em hills now. Now! One of 'em is ya behind Anazet even thou ya behind is pretendin it ain't in the group!

*(***SINGING RAIN*** hands* **SAVANNA** *water)*

SAVANNA. Thanks…Rain.

DINAH. *(nearly out of control)* Did you hear me? We–

HONEY. DINAH!

DINAH. Dinah, my velvet ass! There's 'nugh blood in that big house to mop alla 'em floors. She cut him like a pig.

ANAZET. –I did nothing!

DINAH. *(absolutely frantic)* Bed, rug, curtains leaking with blood! There be blood in them winds now. We got to stay 'head! We got to go! We got to go!!

SAVANNA. Where? Go where without direction?

DINAH. Outta these parts now!

SAVANNA. *(struggling to stay in control)* They won't find him 'til morning.

DINAH. Maybe they will, maybe not.

SAVANNA. Rest horses, git direction, then run till we there.

DINAH. I say run them horses now, take our chances!

BULLET. See what you let stay?

SINGING RAIN. *(ignoring)* I can't hear ya.

CONCHATA. I like 'em.

BULLET. Ya like bugs.

DINAH. *(out of control)* Why can't we? WHY CAN'T WE?

SAVANNA. I give ya three reasons. Margaret…James and–

HONEY. –Baby Ada.

(silence/pause)

SAVANNA. Mark us all, night they run.

HONEY. And circle back in the rope.

SAVANNA. They run. They lost. Just plain out roped 'em. But now with us-

HONEY. Won't be that kinda simple. *(to SAVANNA)* Then ya got some answers to git. I ain't woke you up so they can put us down.

DINAH. *(quietly rattled, desperate fear)* Do somethin', Honey.

HONEY. *(to sister "tough" assurance)* We make it, always do. What you say?

(quietly between the sisters)

DINAH. I'm wit ya.

HONEY. Right beside ya, all round ya.

DINAH/HONEY. I'm wit ya.

SINGING RAIN. *(thinking)* Blood in the wind.

SAVANNA. Miss Bullet?

(BULLET deliberately sighing.)

HONEY. It's true, ya can hear things 'fore it get here? That true?

SINGING RAIN. Sometimes.

CONCHATA. *(child-cheerful, proud)* I hear you comin'!

DINAH. *(referring to trap door)* Hell, ya can probably hear a bug shit down there.

HONEY. How I'm gon' tell somebody ridin' up 'fore they git here?

CONCHATA. The earth tell ya.

SAVANNA. *(rapid command)* Check the outsides, four corners, hitch em' closer, saddle off MyZion.

(HONEY and DINAH exchange looks)

HONEY. Saddle off?

SAVANNA. –go 'head. *(whispers)*

(DINAH is glaring at ANAZET. SAVANNA notices.)

SAVANNA. Dinah! Cover ya sista, I want ya in that tree.

DINAH. Me? Tree? Snakes!

SAVANNA. Rather it be men?

DINAH. *(stalling)* I git water first.

BULLET. *(to* **HONEY***)* Ya can tell by listenin', but ya got to listen like a tree.

DINAH. *(whispering to* **HONEY***)* Listen like a tree, hell she talkin' 'bout? *(pause)* Think she drinks?

HONEY. Drinks what out here?

DINAH. Tree sap or somethin'…

(**SAVANNA** *notices* **CONCHATA** *staring at her pants.*)

SAVANNA. You must be Raindrop.

CONCHATA. My name's Conchata. Ya wear bottoms.

SAVANNA. For ridin'.

(There is a crack outside. The women freeze. **SAVANNA** *hitches up her pants to reveal a knife strapped to her leg. She un-straps it. Then tosses it to* **HONEY.** **SINGING RAIN** *and* **BULLET** *position their guns.* **SAVANNA** *gently but swiftly extends her open hand.)*

SAVANNA. Miss Bullet, my word, I give it back.

(**BULLET** *stares, then tosses her gun.*)

SAVANNA. *(To* **ANAZET***)* Git over here.

SINGING RAIN. Conchata.

(**CONCHATA** *disappointingly backs away.* **ANAZET** *does not move.*)

SAVANNA. Ya rather I come git ya?

SINGING RAIN. *(to* **CONCHATA***)* Go in.

CONCHATA. *(softly protesting)* Momma.

SINGING RAIN. Go!

(**CONCHATA** *returns to the trap door.* **ANAZET** *crosses to* **SAVANNA** *who grabs her to the front door holding a gun on her but not to her head.* **SINGING RAIN** *and* **BULLET** *station near the trap door.*)

(silence)

(**HONEY** *begins to exit.*)

DINAH. *(worried)* Honey...

HONEY. Come on. You got to listen like a tree. *(No joke.)*

(**HONEY** and **DINAH** exit.)

ANAZET. He'll take you down with me.

SAVANNA. Then you best not go down.

ANAZET. I can tell him–

SAVANNA. Ya can tell 'em what I want ya to tell 'em, now cut it! *(pause)* What ya mean "he"? Who ya talkin' 'bout?

ANAZET. His brother, Jeremiah. If he should find me...let him find me dead.

HONEY. *(offstage:)* Savanna!

SAVANNA. Honey?

DINAH. *(offstage:)* Aint nothin'.

SAVANNA. *(trying to reassure her)* We got an edge on 'em. *(quiet thought to **ANAZET**)* ...Jeremiah? He ain't right in the head.

ANAZET. Yet they'll follow him like money. He'll get a hunt.

DINAH. *(offstage:)* Y'all all right?

(**DINAH** quickly enters, checks and exits.)

SAVANNA. *(To **ANAZET**)* What he got on you?

(**CONCHATA** has snuck back out the trap door. **SAVANNA** releases **ANAZET**, hands **BULLET** her gun and notices **CONCHATA**. **SAVANNA** takes off a little wooden bracelet and hands it to **CONCHATA**.)

SAVANNA. Ya like this?

(**CONCHATA** smiles and shakes her head yes. She looks at her mother, and her mother nods yes.)

CONCHATA. Thank you.

SAVANNA. Cherry wood, I made it.

(**CONCHATA** runs to the trap door and brings out a little bird made of branches. She hands it to **SAVANNA**.)

CONCHATA. Like it?

SAVANNA. Yep.

CONCHATA. Singing branches, I made it. Some trees sing. Hold my bird high, she sings.

(**CONCHATA** *flies the bird high running round the shelter singing then glides it to* **SAVANNA**.)

CONCHATA. For you.

SAVANNA. Can't keep it, thank ya the same.

CONCHATA. *(gently protesting)* I made it.

SAVANNA. Sorry. Ain't used to–. Thank ya.

(**SAVANNA** *makes a spectacle of herself trying to find a safe place on her body to put her gift. She notices everyone watching, stops and just holds it in her hand.* **HONEY** *enters.*)

SAVANNA. Git the horses. Tell Dinah loose the saddles, bring MyZion's saddles in. You got 'nough water for 'em and you tonight?

SINGING RAIN. Yes.

SAVANNA. Water 'em, walk 'em a bit, see if they'll feed.

HONEY. Ya want me to kiss goodnight, too?

SAVANNA. Just do-

(*In a moment* **SAVANNA** *is frozen and silent. All the women are listening intently. They freeze.* **SAVANNA** *crosses to the door and watches animal still. Total silence.*)

SAVANNA. *(to* **BULLET***)* Miss Bullet, I'll hand it back.

(**SAVANNA** *extends her arm for a gun.* **BULLET** *slowly gives it to her.* **SAVANNA** *scouts with her eyes. She exits and enters with* **DINAH**. *She hands the gun back to* **BULLET**. *The women are slightly relieved.* **BULLET** *and* **RAIN** *continue their talk extremely aware of their surroundings.*)

SAVANNA. Hurry back.

HONEY. *(to* **DINAH***)* What you see? (**DINAH** *nervously shakes her head 'nothing'*) We ain't strapped. (**HONEY** *and* **DINAH** *look at* **SAVANNA***)*

SAVANNA. *(looking at* **BULLET***)* Use your senses.

DINAH. That tree thing again…

> (**BULLET** *unexpectedly tosses gun at* **HONEY** *who sharply catches. Both women show impressive skill.* **HONEY** *nods to* **BULLET**. *The sisters exit. After* **SAVANNA** *covers them with her eyes, slightly satisfied, she returns to shelter.)*

ANAZET. What are you planning on doing with me?

SAVANNA. They ain't said.

ANAZET. They 'are' coming for me.

> (**BULLET** *and* **RAIN** *look at one another.)*

SAVANNA. *(trying to evade conversation)* Ain't got use for that talk now.

ANAZET. No use for the truth?

SAVANNA. *(talking to* **ANAZET** *to reassure* **BULLET** *and* **RAIN***)* I covered the tracks.

ANAZET. Let me go. What Mister did was not part of my doing.

SAVANNA. But it parta ya undoin'.

ANAZET. I'll throw them off. I will play as if I escaped on my own. They will not have to know you let me go. I can even pay for your help. I have one hidden box of silver left and I had nothing to do with Charlotte. He never spoke of her to me. Dinah killed him, she did it. I only tried to stop her.

SAVANNA. That why there's blood on ya, too?

ANAZET. I was there, that is all. It was in my own bedroom after all.

SAVANNA. He still there?

> (**ANAZET** *shakes her head yes.)*

SAVANNA. Who wakes ya?

ANAZET. I do not allow anyone in my bedroom!

SAVANNA. Mister did.

ANAZET. Well, I don't…didn't. Bethanne won't disturb my, the room, unless I open my, the door. *(to herself-unbelievably)* It's over…I won't return.

SAVANNA. Was it shut?

(**ANAZET** *shrugs her shoulders.*)

SAVANNA. If you ain't killed him, you musta liked what he did to ya. I ain't figured you'd like it.

ANAZET. *(indignant)* I don't know what you are speaking of.

SAVANNA. Ain't nobody fool. Ya got the clothes on your back, just like the rest of us.

ANAZET. I am not like the rest of you! And do you really believe that is all I will ever have, just like the rest of you?

SAVANNA. Won't even be your life, ya keep yappin'.

ANAZET. My offer stands.

BULLET. How far you ride?

SAVANNA. Five, six hours. But they won't find him, 'till after day break.

ANAZET. Humpf!

BULLET. You so sure?

SINGING RAIN. Why?

SAVANNA. Every night, he sleep in different quarters. Come day break, and she get up–

ANAZET. –Keep my name out of this!

SAVANNA. And she up, he goes to the big house, sleep it off. They shut the door, that way they won't find him when he start to smell.

BULLET. What's your last name child?

SAVANNA. –I

(**BULLET** *freezes. The shelter freezes.* **SAVANNA** *quickly checks the outsides. She does not exit.*)

SAVANNA. Honey?

HONEY. We all right.

SAVANNA. *(to* **BULLET***)* Savanna's all I got.

BULLET. How'd ya find me?

SAVANNA. Folks speak ya name with admiration.

BULLET. You ain't rode this far to admire.

SAVANNA. I been 'round ya once.

BULLET. How's that?

SAVANNA. Round spring. Had to git me fresh horses. Thomasville. You 'bout six more hidin' in a cattle car.

SINGING RAIN. John. My John.

SAVANNA. *(not a question)* You the one start to birth.

SINGING RAIN. Thomasville.

BULLET. 'Bout got us caught if it ain't for them horses.

SAVANNA. I pictured what come next. Lucky thing ya train car near to the horse car, that way when I pulled the latch, their poundin' off shut out her birthin' cries.

(**BULLET** *and* **RAIN** *stare startled at* **SAVANNA.**)

BULLET. That was you?

SAVANNA. Yes, Ma'am.

SINGING RAIN. Horses run 'cause of you?

BULLET. In the next car?

SINGING RAIN. Spirit send you. I pray Spirit help us, help us. Spirit send you.

BULLET. Nobody seen ya?

SAVANNA. No, Ma'am. No.

BULLET. They always huntin' us in them cars, nobody-

SAVANNA. Well….they…see I, I…

(**SAVANNA** *is visibly shaken.*)

BULLET. *(gently with knowing understanding)* Ya ain't got to say.

SAVANNA. Maybe there is Spirit, like ya said.

SINGING RAIN. You pray?

SAVANNA. Once.

BULLET. Why you stop?

SAVANNA. 'Cause my prayer. I ain't really know what I was doin'. Truth is I ain't even know who I was talkin' to. Just words really. Hard, scared words that after they dropped me. I's still breathin'. Never touched it again.

SINGING RAIN. …Dropped you? Dropped you?

ANAZET. You've been hung?!

(pause - clearly yes)

BULLET.	**RAIN.**
Have mercy.	Oh, Spirit.

SAVANNA. ...don't know why I'm breathin'. Guess that's the sign I been runnin' round after. Never had chance to say I think highly of ya. Heard stories of what you been doing. Well, there ain't never been much to me. But that time in Thomasville was chance to change that. When I pulled the latch, horses lit off, they saw. I ran. Men chased me, ran me down with their own horses. I been trying to find work. That's why I came. I can do most anything with a horse. Birth 'em, calm 'em, ride 'em, nudge out their strengths. Be surprised--their smarts, got ways a talkin' to ya too. Thomasville's horse country. I figured it held something for me... life folds on ya sometimes. They caught me, done me in. When they roped the tree, strung me up on that horse naked, something' in me got still. Maybe there's Spirit somewhere, you know, somewhere that I don't know nothin' 'bout, 'cause when they spooked that horse, I yanked up, Spirit caught my neck with wind, kept me live, even after I's dropped. Was Honey and Dinah cut me off, cared for me, healed me up 'till I could make word again. They ain't killed me. But I never spirit talked again.

BULLET. Do Jesus.

SAVANNA. *(to* **BULLET***)* Been keeping' up wit ya. Ain't known what I'm hoping for, 'cept maybe now, start fresh, me and my new sistas.

SINGING RAIN. Spirit won't hurt ya. Pray again. Pray again, Savanna.

CONCHATA. My mother says, always pray. We come to the morning with our Love for you Creator. Thank you for my breath. Thank you for the new morning, and for the sky. Thank you for my sister brother birds, thank you for my mother, and for my mother Bullet–

CONCHATA and **SINGING RAIN**. –I give you my Love, Creator.

CONCHATA. You pray for ya horses?

SINGING RAIN. *(to* **BULLET***)* Tell her. Go with her.

BULLET. *(suddenly agitated)* And leave ya?

CONCHATA. We can't leave ya, Momma.

BULLET. We been round this and round this-

SINGING RAIN. -And you don't listen.

BULLET. You don't listen!

CONCHATA. Don't fight.

SINGING RAIN. My time comes.

BULLET. How ya know?

SINGING RAIN. John tells me.

BULLET. Well, he ain't told me.

SINGING RAIN. Because he talks to me!

>   (**CONCHATA** *and* **SAVANNA** *dialogue nearly overlaps* **SINGING RAIN** *and* **BULLET***)*

CONCHATA. *(louder)* Don't fight. *(whispers to* **SAVANNA***)* John is my father. They kill him.

SAVANNA. Sorry.

BULLET. I keep telling' ya we can make it in the hills, pass the mountains, it's the river what we got to pray at.

>   (**SAVANNA** *is taking mental notes.*)

SAVANNA. Ah, Miss Bullet, why the river?

>   (**BULLET** *and* **SINGING RAIN** *do not respond.*)

CONCHATA. *(to* **SAVANNA***)* Snakes. The water under the water pulls this way and that way. *(She demonstrates a rough current with her hands.)* River lets some 'cross her, others no… (**CONCHATA** *points her fingers to show drowning*). And snakes.

SINGING RAIN.	**BULLET.**
My prayers cover you and Conchata.	We ain't leaving wit out ya.

CONCHATA. *(nervously)* Don't leave us, Momma.

(**SINGING RAIN** *glares at* **BULLET** *for upsetting* **CONCHATA**.*)*

SINGING RAIN. You need to 'see' our daughter grows old waiting to grow.

BULLET. *(angry)* Then go on, tell her 'bout how you and John gon' fly home.

(**BULLET** *angrily storms to the door about to exit but is stopped.*)

SINGING RAIN. You use me.

(**BULLET** *halts at door. The room is silent.*)

BULLET. *(surprise/disbelief)* What?

(**BULLET** *and* **SINGING RAIN** *quietly have a verbal stand off, a different kind of stand-off.* **SAVANNA** *quietly but quickly rises to her feet motioning* **ANAZET** *to do the same. It could get rough(er).* **ANAZET** *understands and rises.* **SAVANNA** *and* **ANAZET** *move to exit but are caught.*)

BULLET. I said, what did you say?

(**BULLET** *moves toward* **SINGING RAIN**. **SINGING RAIN** *rises not a hint of weakness.*)

SINGING RAIN. You use me and give Conchata danger.

(**SAVANNA** *and* **ANAZET** *remain caught.*)

BULLET. After all I–

SINGING RAIN. –You scared.

(**SAVANNA** *halts but does not look at* **BULLET**. *Speech intense and quiet.*)

SINGING RAIN. –and you use me to stay scared.

CONCHATA. *(quietly, nervously)* Don't fight…

BULLET. I done pulled trees from the earth, moved-

SINGING RAIN. –a cloud from the sun but not a foot to be free. We bury John. I lose my baby. Now you scared. Lift the river, lift it, no more scared.

*(The following is **BULLET** and **SINGING RAIN** talking to each other through a somewhat embarrassed **SAVANNA**.)*

BULLET. *(to **SAVANNA**, who is trying not to be there)* She know you can't cross them waters.

SINGING RAIN. *(to **SAVANNA**)* But with her *(referring to **BULLET**)* you can.

BULLET. You can't! Not in forwards, nor back, rock everywhere. Water dip over ya head in a sudden. All directions at once. Ya gotta move what way the river, she wants.

SAVANNA. What ways that?

BULLET. If I knew would we hide here?

SINGING RAIN. *(to **SAVANNA**)* She know. *(referring to **BULLET**)*

SAVANNA. *(to **BULLET**)* Show me.

SINGING RAIN. *(to **SAVANNA**)* You follow.

BULLET. No stars. Horses won't go

SINGING RAIN. Go mornin'. My prayers cover ya.

BULLET. Damnit, no! I can't leave ya! Would you leave me?

SINGING RAIN. This, my path, not yours.

BULLET. Well then, I best find my own path.

CONCHATA. Mother Bullet.

SINGING RAIN. Now I hear you.

*(**BULLET** storms out, exits past a frozen **SAVANNA** and **ANAZET**)*

*(**SINGING RAIN** looks at an angry **CONCHATA**. **DINAH**'s head peeks in.)*

DINAH. Anybody dead?

*(**SAVANNA**'s face speaks: a non-verbal, "Get back outside." **DINAH**'s reply is also in her face, a non-verbal, "Just checkin'.")*

*(**DINAH** exits. **SAVANNA** remains by the door watching. **ANAZET** moves about the shelter but does not sit back down. Her back hurts her.)*

SINGING RAIN. *(to herself outloud)* Wind catch your throat, but no wind for my John.

SAVANNA. Sorry.

SINGING RAIN. *(to* **CONCHATA***)* What did you see?

CONCHATA. Momma Bullet hides me in skirt. I can't see Papa...you always ask me.

SINGING RAIN. You always tell me.

CONCHATA. *(bright idea)* But I see you and Papa in the water one day with no clothes on.

SINGING RAIN. *(taken by surprise)* WHAT?

(The women look up and at her. **SINGING RAIN** *is embarrassed and* **CONCHATA** *is pleased it worked.)*

CONCHATA. I said, I see you and Father–

SINGING RAIN. –I hear you!

(Pause. **CONCHATA** *and* **RAIN** *smile.)*

SINGING RAIN. Come. *(motions to* **SAVANNA***)*

*(***SAVANNA** *walks to* **RAIN** *and sits beside her)*

The hills. *(***RAIN** *touches* **SAVANNA***'s forehead)* The mountains. *(She touches her cheekbones.)* The rivers. *(She touches her mouth.)* The water quiet, beautiful. If snakes don't git ya the water under the water will. Pray, then 'cross. The hills, the mountains, the waters...and my daughter.

*(***SAVANNA** *looks at* **CONCHATA** *who is near tears, then at* **SINGING RAIN***, deeply thinking exits.)*

SINGING RAIN. My daughter, you will *have*.

CONCHATA. Will I have my mother?

SINGING RAIN. Mother Bullet is right, I don't know that moment but it comes soon.

ANAZET. You have a beautiful little girl.

SINGING RAIN. You have children?

ANAZET. Just myself.

CONCHATA. Are you sad?

ANAZET. Not with a little girl like you about.

*(***SAVANNA** *is on the outside of shelter,* **HONEY** *enters.)*

HONEY. Where's Anazet?

SAVANNA. Inside. Where's Bullet?

HONEY. Over yonder.

SAVANNA. Dinah?

HONEY. Other side. She forgets how to think, when she under me…Make me scared for her.

(**HONEY** *and* **SAVANNA** *stay near the door listening for* **DINAH.**)

(*pause*)

HONEY. I been seein' Charlotte, ain't I?

(**SAVANNA** *looks away.*)

HONEY. Yeah. (*pause*) After we 'cross that river-

SAVANNA. (*firm*) I'm gon' bring y'all through.

HONEY. Yeah. (*politely unconvinced*) I do too see Charlotte. 'Times I just don't say nothin', she smile soft like, then… Singing Rain know, lots do…I suppose. (*pause*) Got this feeling, after we cross–

SAVANNA. –You'll done brought me out. That's what on my mind, branches crackin' 'cross my face, circlin', twistin', duckin'…it's me sayin' thank you. Come off MyZion pee round trees, throw the dogs if they bring 'em. Wild dreams got to chasin' me again. I make myself make it. You all washed me, wet my bread, stood wit me. I pee round 'em trees 'till I had nothin' left. Rode MyZion front ways and back, throwin' pepper on the path, we goin' through.

(**HONEY** *is understanding and softly unconvinced.* **SAVANNA**, *aware, enters the shelter.* **HONEY** *curiously enters behind her.*)

SAVANNA. Singing Rain, what mountains? Everywhere's mountains. Tell me or we'll circle back in 'em ropes.

SINGING RAIN. I show you what I know. But she knows. Conchata.

SAVANNA. Send Dinah in.

(**HONEY** *opens door* **DINAH** *immediately appears carrying the saddle.*)

HONEY. Thought I left you round back.

(**DINAH** *enters.* **SAVANNA, SINGING RAIN, CONCHATA** *exit.*)

DINAH. Where y'all goin'?

HONEY. Get answers.

DINAH. How you doin' with that blood in ya nails, Anazet?

ANAZET. Far better than you'll be doing in the end.

DINAH. Not this time. I'm-

(There is a loud sound again like a crack. The women freeze. Pause. From outside of the shelter **SAVANNA** *calls.)*

SAVANNA. It's all right.

(**HONEY** *has remained in the freeze.*)

DINAH. Honey..? Honey..?!

HONEY. Told her not to go out. Never leave me. Where is she?

DINAH. She's in the field, picking berries for ya.

HONEY. In the field? Somebody took her in the fields?

DINAH. *(impatient and nervous)* Please come outta there!

HONEY. Charlotte?

DINAH. Come outta there!

HONEY. Charlotte? Don't you never leave out alone. Dinah?!

DINAH. I'm here!

(**HONEY** *suddenly drills her sister on survival.*)

HONEY. What moon we move by?

DINAH. What? Ah, full yella.

HONEY. What star we walk wit?

DINAH. East Star.

HONEY. Hungry?

DINAH. Low vine, black fruit.

HONEY. Bleeding?

DINAH. Stuff privates with leaves.

HONEY. Sleep?

DINAH. Trees, caves, swamps

HONEY. Dogs?

DINAH. Pee circles.

HONEY. Waters?

DINAH. Waters?

HONEY. Rivers? RIVERS!!!

DINAH. I…I…

HONEY. How you gon' make it, if ya don't know water?

DINAH. I forgot.

HONEY. How?

*(**HONEY** charges over to slap **DINAH**.)*

DINAH. Honey! No. I 'member, I 'member! Moccasins! Look for signs of moccasins.

HONEY. Don't you never forget.

*(**DINAH** goes to fetch **HONEY** water and realizes they are alone with **ANAZET**. **DINAH** looks around the shelter as if to be sure. **HONEY** collapses then holds her head. **DINAH** glares at **ANAZET**. **ANAZET** realizes too, she is alone with **DINAH**.)*

DINAH. What you do wit her?

ANAZET. You should know what happened after he put you in the field. After you didn't please him anymore.

DINAH. How it feel being colored, playing white, whipped a slave?

ANAZET. That last part you can tell me.

DINAH. I a woman wit freedom.

ANAZET. Not in my bedroom. I am willing to bet that's not what you were up in my bedroom.

DINAH. Is that why you killed him?

ANAZET. Is that why you killed him?

DINAH. Yeah, I killed him 'cause I ain't stopped ya.

ANAZET. Mule-headed nigra!

DINAH. Red worm witch! You ever been on the block?

ANAZET. Find a porch and sleep under it!

(**DINAH** *has gotten up and moved to the saddle where the rope is.*)

HONEY. *(still dazed, in and out)* You sold my baby off? You put her on the block, ain't ya?

ANAZET. I don't know what Mister did.

(**DINAH** *is moving to* **ANAZET** *with the saddle and rope.*)

HONEY. What they do with my baby? What they do? They wash her like a horse, check in her mouth, check in her head? Did they check my baby? Don't touch her! Don't touch her!

DINAH. *(moves toward* **ANAZET***)* You been checked?

ANAZET. Dirty wash bucket nigras, get away from me. I'll have ya horse whipped for this.

(**HONEY** *and* **DINAH** *move closer and closer.*)

HONEY. NOW!

(**HONEY** *and* **DINAH** *grab* **ANAZET**. *They put the rope around her neck, stuff her mouth and twist her abstractly with the rope. They put her on an imaginary auction block then perform an auction.* **HONEY** *is half in trance but not slow in rhythm.*)

DINAH. Now Ladies and Gentlemen–

HONEY. –She can carry water–

DINAH. We come to the children.

HONEY. –pick berries–

DINAH. –We have with us today–

HONEY. –feed the feeble–

DINAH. –a lil nigress for sale.

HONEY. –A play toy for your child–

DINAH. –when your dogs are busy–

HONEY. –ya can pet her instead–

DINAH. –be your footstool–

HONEY. –sleep on your bed floor–
DINAH. One lil sweet child!–
HONEY. –Pretty lil nigress for sale!
DINAH. Biddin' open!

*(With each chore **DINAH** has twisted **ANAZET** into grotesque positions representing a child performing those chores. **ANAZET** is in serious pain.)*

*(**SAVANNA** enters bursting)*

SAVANNA. I can hear ya clear out –What ya doin'?

*(**SAVANNA** notices the rope around **ANAZET**'s neck. They immediately stop and drop the rope.)*

SAVANNA. *(has a reaction to the rope on her neck)* Take the rope off her. Take it off her neck!

*(**HONEY** is dazed and, in deep thought, exits. **DINAH** takes her time in obeying.)*

*(**RAIN**, **CONCHATA**, and **BULLET** enter shelter wondering what the noise was. **BULLET** hands **DINAH** some leaves. **DINAH** is confused.)*

BULLET. *(to **DINAH**)* For ya sista. Let it sit in her jaw. Might help.

*(**DINAH** exits surprised and appreciative.)*

SAVANNA. *(to **BULLET** and **RAIN**)* I'm at the door.

*(**SAVANNA** exits outside door, not knowing **CONCHATA** has slipped out with her. Exit **CONCHATA**. Lights down on exterior shelter except for the boots of **SAVANNA** and **CONCHATA**/ **SINGING RAIN** notices **ANAZET**'s back, quietly alerts **BULLET**.)*

SINGING RAIN. *(to **ANAZET**)* Blood on your back.

*(**BULLET** and **SINGING RAIN** exchange looks).*

BULLET. Ya want somethin' for it?
ANAZET. I don't know what to want.

(**BULLET** *and* **SINGING RAIN** *cross to inspect her back, again exchange looks recognizing the marks.*)

BULLET. It's fresh.

SINGING RAIN. *(She examines it, slightly confused.)* No…they don't beat ya?

ANAZET. Not them.

(**BULLET** *and* **SINGING RAIN** *exchange looks again.*)

BULLET. Don't have much, but I got somethin' for it.

(**BULLET** *crosses to fetch her herbs.*)

ANAZET. My husband.

(**BULLET** *and* **SINGING RAIN** *pause.*)

BULLET. *(halts, but not greatly surprised)* Your husband?

SINGING RAIN. *(surprised)* …your husband in big house?

(**ANAZET** *admits with somewhat shameful and stunned silence.*)

BULLET. Lotta things go on in 'em houses…wit everybody.

(**ANAZET** *shakes her head yes.* **ANAZET** *looks out, mostly speaking to herself.*)

(*Lights slightly dim. Tree branches create leaf patterns in shelter across* **ANAZET** *as she speaks.* **BULLET**, **SINGING RAIN** *and the tree listen in the shadows.*)

ANAZET. I had this notion…I had this notion to look into the books. At first I couldn't find them. Mister told me that once we became man and wife he would take care of me, take care of everything. Still, I had this notion to look into the books. When finally I retrieved them, they were most inaccurate. I never kept my books like that. However, one thing was very clear, we were losing money and had been losing it for a long time. I had seen the signs but…He was buying building materials, buying more help, horses, saddles, feed and why? We made– I made this money from…That evening, I dreamt of my first day ever of buying land, holding that deed in my gloves, acquiring property, my own home, a sizeable dwelling and help, my first chest of silver, my triumph, all of it, swallowed in blood. In the morning, when he stumbled out of one of the quarters, as always, this time I didn't hold my tongue. I opened the book and pointed out to him what I had read. He straightened up the way snakes can, eyes growing large and it was then that I had forgotten that I wasn't a man. He said, ya ever question me again, I'll beat ya like a nigga. And then I saw it, the mistake I had wed, this heap of flesh smelling woman privates. I didn't run from the room because of what he had said to me. I ran because I couldn't smell him anymore. And one day I became scared, it seemed after that he really started spending. And I, I questioned him again…I had to, and he kept his promise. The next morning I had lumps in my tongue from where I had bitten down on it. I tried not to scream so the help wouldn't know he's whipping me like a nigga. He tore my shirt blouse, bent me down and split my back open, just like a nigga. I bought that land, the help and my first chest of silver…my triumph, and he beat me like I was just nothing. But that was the last time he was ever to raise a hand to me and I kept my own promise.

(pause)

SINGING RAIN. Ya woman with freedom now.

*(**CONCHATA** quietly enters. She is carrying stones and twigs. She puts them on the floor to play leaning on the tree.)*

ANAZET. I can't leave here.

BULLET. Won't be forever.

*(**BULLET** prepares her herbs for **ANAZET** pulling leaves from the tree and branches hanging from the walls, bundles in baskets working steady quietly clear knowing what she's doing.)*

ANAZET. What good is being free when you're hunted?

BULLET. What's the good when captured up?

(**ANAZET** *notices* **CONCHATA** *playing and staring at her.*)

ANAZET. *(to* **SINGING RAIN***)* May I meet your little girl? She keeps looking at me.

SINGING RAIN. She looks at your cloth. Maybe she 'sees' in you.

(**SINGING RAIN** *nods to* **CONCHATA**. **CONCHATA** *walks to* **ANAZET**. **SINGING RAIN** *and* **BULLET** *mix herbs, wet them in bucket to place them on* **ANAZET***'s back. They both go to the tree and whisper prayers holding the basket to the tree during following dialogue.*)

ANAZET. Hello, princess.

(**ANAZET** *extends her hand.* **CONCHATA** *stares at her ring.*)

ANAZET. You have excellent taste.

CONCHATA. It's pretty.

ANAZET. My triumph. Winner. It's very, very special. *(Gently, questioningly,* **CONCHATA** *tries to remove ring.)* No princess, I had better keep this. But you can wear this. Would you like to?

(**CONCHATA** *to her mother waiting until they finish praying. Then points to necklace.* **SINGING RAIN** *nods yes.* **ANAZET** *places it around a happy* **CONCHATA**. **CONCHATA** *stares at the buttons on* **ANAZET***'s blouse.* **DINAH** *enters fetching water.*)

CONCHATA. They're seeds.

ANAZET. They're pearls from the ocean.

CONCHATA. Like the moon. Like moon seeds.

ANAZET. These are the only seeds I have now. I don't have seeds, *(to herself)* not any that could grow with him… thank my God. Here you keep this.

(**ANAZET** *pulls a button off her blouse and hands it to* **CONCHATA**. **HONEY** *enters.* **SINGING RAIN** *and* **BULLET** *place herb leaves on her aching back. Sensitive,* **ANAZET** *fights back obvious pain.*)

DINAH. But, you gon' have velvet, little princess. French lace and pearls, just like her husband used to try and give me. 'Cept yours gon' be better 'cause you gon' buy 'em for your own liking, not 'cause somebody tryin' to buy your likin'.

CONCHATA. I'm gonna have more pearls?

DINAH. And this here tiny flower. Ain't it pretty? *(hands* **CONCHATA** *night bloom)*

CONCHATA. Mother, it's pretty.

DINAH. Ain't got nothin' on ya.

CONCHATA. I never seen it.

HONEY. Night bloom.

DINAH. You gon' have a right smart horse–

CONCHATA. –like MyZion?!

DINAH. –and a great, big, happy house. That's what I want.

CONCHATA. *(Just so happy. She throws arms wide open.)* Me too! We all gon' live in my house, together!

(CONCHATA happily looks around at everyone. Pause. They all quietly look around at one another like that will never happen)

DINAH. *(nearly to herself–unknowing premonition)* You won't see me, but I'll see you.

(SAVANNA enters holding her neck. HONEY notices.)

SAVANNA. *(to* **ANAZET***)* Come on, relieve yourself.

HONEY. What's got ya?

SAVANNA. Don't know.

(ANAZET, SAVANNA exit. CONCHATA quietly slips out.)

BULLET. You all work for her husband?

HONEY. Used to dance wit a carnival. Mister pay the carnival man and us too, real silver to come off it. Said we be his parlor show for business times. Thought that be better for my lil girl, Charlotte…and Savanna. Maybe my Charlotte could have learning. Might somebody know readin'. And Savanna could heal up more.

Seems like we all been together for long time. We women with freedom…but it different kinda freedom.

DINAH. Honey always say, watch him, git 'hind me, watch him.

BULLET. Always the flesh.

DINAH. 'Cause she could see his insides. Then one day he call me out…wanta see me good.

HONEY. Ya was untouched.

DINAH. Be that way still! 'Cause before it was always you.

HONEY. Don't talk 'bout it. Ya hear me?

(HONEY shakes her head knowing DINAH has to get it out.)

(DINAH is half talking to herself and half reliving it. She is not truly talking to the women. Lights on DINAH dim in shelter creating a different leaf pattern on DINAH. It is a pretty, light feeling almost spring.)

DINAH. First time he called me to him: Bring me the horse's whip, I want it with us. I ain't never really been what I'd seen whipped. I been slapped, shoved, had to take spittle, but I ain't never been, like my sister been. I picked it up from the horse's stalls, all while thinkin', what he gon' do…? What he gon' do to me? I started to float feeling fear. What he gon' do? I hope he don't whip my women parts, I hope he don't whip my face, I hope…what he gon' do? I come up to the big fat sun peeing bedroom, 'cause that's where he wants this. I'm a woman wit freedom, my sister bought me, what he gon' do? He wants it right where they sleep, or supposed to. Bed look like its sitting on a cloud and I'm somewhere in trick heaven. His eyes start growing. "Over here" he say. He twist and whine a wad of cloth in his fist like he gon' stuff that in my mouth. He smell the whip like some low animal. I use this on the others, he opened his shirt, said: I want you to use it on me. He takes my arm, yanks it up. Come on, hard now.

(pause)

DINAH. I'm thinkin', this must be white folk Christmas, I'm gon' get to whip up on a white man? He stuff the cloth in his own mouth. He can't be talkin' to me, must be somebody 'hind me, slipped in when I wasn't lookin' 'cause last looking I am colored and colored don't whip up on no white...not like this. I'm still standing there with my arm in a big "how do?" with a whip at the end of it. He said, if I don't whip him, he gon' whip me.

(pause)

I tried to whip him to death. I was pantin' trying to whip the hell out his pink dotted white ass. I popped that ass so hard it blew up like a cloud. He took it like a mule. I learned to draw blood, rip new flesh, and even make infections. I never let a wound heal. Once, with his eye growing he put his face to me, whip in his spitty mouth, and told me, lick it. I ain't moved gots to thinkin' if he ever put his mouth on me, I'd kill him. He musta heard me thinkin' 'cause he said, if you ever stop, I'll do the killing. So I whipped him from winter to spring. Come spring, he wanta build new barns, start trading more horses, just spending. He renting some coloreds from nearby county. Esau was one of 'em. Strong and wonderful colored man. He smiled at me and I smiled back. I brought me a big feeling home one day. Honey was the first to see it. Why 'm thinkin' of him now? I didn't think I'd think of him again. His man softness, a first real touch. He used to bring me flowers on his back. He'd hide 'em on his skin. He'd have honeysuckle and roses stuck to his back. Bowed to me and say, for you. I'd peel 'em off just like he was fruit. You'd think a strong man like him, sweating, worked too hard, that they'd be stinkin' flowers. They'd always be sweet and he'd be a huge smell of honeysuckle roses. I'd plant a touch where I took each petal, like a thank you. I used to dream how he'd be my very firstest kiss, before the day we both stole time together, to touch and place our arms round one another. To laugh a bit and then I looked into his eyes and they started to grow. Don't know when I said, take off your shirt, don't know when I broke branch off the tree, raised my arm and brought it down. He caught it. Somethin' musta been runnin' in my eyes, he said just as soft, is this what they done to you? Is this what they done to you? I closed his shirt. He close his heart? I could hear 'em callin' for all the boys. He took his palm to my small beating heart. It was the last day. Some came back to finish up, not him. Once I think I saw him again, but I dropped my head. Told myself, I wouldn't whip nothin' no more. I might kill something but I ain't gon' whip nothin' no more and right after, Honey started callin', where's Charlotte? I can't find Charlotte. And Mister never did call me up again... *(slowly lights come up)* Is this what they done to you? How come I remember him now?

HONEY. 'Cause somewhere he got memory with ya. He never forgot your hand on his back and the tiny feel of petals peeling away from his skin. He carries your touch in his veins. He bends over chops wood and feels your laughter as you take flowers from his shoulders. 'Times at night he turns over and he can feel the last stem being lifted from his neck. He can still feel your heart throbbing like a bird on his fingertips. Mornings, he wakes with all your dream kisses. He thinks he sees where he was sleeping, full of rose petals. He won't never lose that big feelin' you feelin' for him.

(The women freeze listening for danger. **SAVANNA** *enters and throws* **ANAZET** *in the shelter.* **CONCHATA** *runs to her mother. Offstage my* **MYZION** *whinnies throughout speeches. He is warning them.)*

SAVANNA. *(confused and a bit shocked)* Somethin' ain't right. But I circled the trees...

BULLET. *(controlled alarm)* What is it?

*(***SAVANNA*** rubs her neck. Offstage,* **MYZION** *continues to warn them.)*

SAVANNA. Ya hear it? MyZion?

HONEY.	**DINAH.**
Hear what?	What ya hearin'?

SAVANNA. *(To* **HONEY.** **BULLET** *makes a move.)* Check the outsides wit me. No, stay here. Get loaded.

BULLET. I know these parts.

HONEY. *(***DINAH** *makes a move)* Stay in here.

(**SAVANNA, BULLET, HONEY** *exit.* **MYZION** *and* **JUDAH** *whinnying louder.*)

CONCHATA. *(Calmly, she is sensing the earth under foot.)* They come for you now.

ANAZET. *(nervous)* No one is coming.

CONCHATA. Yes, they come. Feel. The earth tells me.

SINGING RAIN. You hear what?

CONCHATA. They come now, Momma.

(**CONCHATA** *lays her body to the floor listening to the earth.* **SINGING RAIN, DINAH,** *and* **ANAZET** *feel the thin wooden/earth floor with their hands.*)

SINGING RAIN. ...and John comes now...

(**SINGING RAIN** *ever so slowly enters a trance.*)

CONCHATA. *(Immediately* **CONCHATA** *is aware.)* Momma!

SINGING RAIN. *(whispers to* **CONCHATA***)* Savanna is a good mother, all your mothers Love you... *(to invisible spirit)* Cover her, John.

CONCHATA. Momma, no, don't go!

SINGING RAIN. You Love me my daughter.

CONCHATA. I'm mad at you! I'm mad at you! No!

SINGING RAIN. You Love me, I know you Love me. I know you give me your life.

ANAZET. *(to* **CONCHATA***)* Get in the door now!

SINGING RAIN. Always pray, we cover you.

(**DINAH** *is trying to drag a seriously fighting* **CONCHATA** *to her trap door)*

CONCHATA. No, No!

DINAH. Come on you gotta go down!

(**CONCHATA** *fights wild, nearly uncontrollable.*)

CONCHATA. I want my mother, my mother!

ANAZET. Be quiet, be quiet.

DINAH. Where are they?

(**DINAH** *seriously struggles with* **CONCHATA**. **ANAZET** *picks up* **DINAH**'s *gun and crosses to the front door.* **DINAH** *has her foot on the trap door as* **CONCHATA** *violently kicks to keep the door open.*)

SINGING RAIN. Where? They run, run…the horses, take it down. I can't see him, take it-

DINAH. *(referring to* **SINGING RAIN***)* Singing Rain help us! Help us! *(to the outsides)* Where are they?

SINGING RAIN. Cover her.

CONCHATA. My mother help me! Mother, don't leave me!

ANAZET. Go down into the door.

CONCHATA. Come get me! Me! Come get me! Momma!

(**SINGING RAIN** *begins spinning about the cabin, knocking things over and digging up the floor.* **ANAZET** *tries to calm her down but gets knocked out the way. She tries again to catch her.*)

ANAZET. Call for Bullet!

DINAH. I can't!

(**ANAZET** *crosses to door opens it as* **BULLET**, **HONEY** *and* **SAVANNA** *rush the shelter.* **BULLET** *immediately attends to* **SINGING RAIN**.*)

SAVANNA. Get your fire!

BULLET. Rain, come on sister, come on…

SAVANNA. *(to* **BULLET***)* GET YA FIRE!!

(**ANAZET** *cracks the door searching for outside signs.*)

ANAZET. *(Not a question)* Oh God. They're coming for me.

SAVANNA. *(to* **ANAZET***)* Get down.

(**ANAZET** *closes the door but does not move.* **BULLET** *returns and has calmed* **SINGING RAIN**.)

SINGING RAIN. Take our daughter. Leave me.

(**BULLET** *quietly talks to* **SINGING RAIN**. **SAVANNA** *suddenly notices that* **ANAZET** *is holding a gun. They both freeze on one another. Pause. All realize the same. The shelter is silent. All eyes remain on* **ANAZET** *during following dialogue.*)

SAVANNA. *(to* **HONEY**) Loaded?

HONEY. Loaded. *(to* **DINAH**) Loaded?

DINAH. Loaded.

SAVANNA. Miss Bullet..?

(**BULLET** *picks up her rifle again as the women hold the weapons on* **ANAZET** *who is moving to the center of shelter. Then they kick what little is in the shelter against the door and position at the windows.* **ANAZET** *remains standing holding the gun.*)

ANAZET. We're outnumbered.

(*For a moment* **ANAZET** *and* **SAVANNA** *are pointing their weapons at one another. Slowly* **ANAZET** *points her weapon out and positions herself on top of* **CONCHATA**'s *trap door. Lights dim on the shelter. The tree creates dark patterns on all the women and shelter. For the first time all natural and outside sound is dead silent.*)

BULLET. *(holds* **SAVANNA**'s *palm in moonlight)* Hand me ya palm. I'm a draw picture map. I lost 'em, 'cause a me, my onliest brother Johnny's gone. Said I never give direction again.

SAVANNA. Ya had done ya best.

BULLET. Held my skirt like wings so she couldn't see the tears, the rope. Remember the waters. I'm gon' draw how to 'cross 'em and listen to ya horses.

SAVANNA. Yes, Ma'am.

BULLET. Pray again.

(**BULLET** *begins drawing a map into the palm of* **SAVANNA***'s hand. It is clear that she is familiar with moonlight.*)

DINAH. Honey…

HONEY. Yeah? *(Pause. Knows what's coming is difficult for* **DINAH.***)* Yeah?

DINAH. I shoulda never stopped–

HONEY. –Don't never be sorry. Never hold ya head low.

DINAH. I kept lookin'.

HONEY. And then what happened?

DINAH. I couldn't move. They'd see and catch us both. I watched over her like my arms be round her. She started to hug herself tight, rockin' and huggin' with all her lil strength. She mutterin', seem like crying. And I can't move.

HONEY. Then…?

DINAH. She got on the lil yellow dress and her arm bones and flesh start pushing out the back, they comin' out her back. I'm watching, can't see how it's happening but her lil bones split her dress cloth, pushing out and up, out and up. I got to get to her. Them bones and flesh be sprouting out her back, painful-like. She muttering loud then she rise up, stops her tears. They comin' out her back, folded and wet and opening. She surprised as I am. In a sudden, I can't see 'cause birds from everywhere landed round us flapping, making rough sound, beating their wings, dust and feathers. Then they leave fast as they come…

HONEY. …And…?

DINAH. –and she gone. Honey, Charlotte is gone. *(pause)* I can run now, but can't see for my own tears. Stumble, pick myself up with her shoe in my hand. You remember how it looks?

HONEY. She gone. Ain't no sense in staying round. I like that story.

DINAH. I'm 'gon make wings one day soon, too.

(**DINAH** *removes the piece of red leather she has hidden on her body and hands it to* **HONEY**.)

HONEY. *(to* **BULLET**/*changing up)* How she comin'?

BULLET. She birthed in a soiled train car. Been runnin', been bleedin' ever since. Worked every root known in these parts. But it's the spirit.

(**SINGING RAIN** *has come to.*)

BULLET. I can't fetch ya no water.

SINGING RAIN. Conchata?

(**BULLET** *nods to floor. Then to* **ANAZET**.)

SAVANNA. Feels like so many.

ANAZET. His brother would lead 'em like this.

HONEY. Like what?

ANAZET. Like snakes. Like the spineless God forsaken thing he is.

HONEY. Maggot brothers.

ANAZET. He once thought he was my husband and forced me to slap his face. He laughed. Kept trying–

DINAH. –What'd you do?

ANAZET. Cut him in his pants. He promised that I'd get mine. That's him coming. Snake.

BULLET. But they're good for soup.

ANAZET. I wouldn't cut his brother up to feed a pig.

SINGING RAIN. Snakes make soup?

BULLET. I never told ya that?

SINGING RAIN. Why I wanta know?

DINAH. I talked to a snake once.

HONEY. She ain't never talk to no snake.

SINGING RAIN. *(joking with her–at a time like this)* A real one?

DINAH. Yep.

BULLET. Or one with two legs?

HONEY. What's the difference?

DINAH. I was lost. He gave direction.

ANAZET. What did he say?

DINAH. Zzzzzay gal? Whazzz ya name? I found home quick.

(They laugh on the inside. Not a chuckle. Maybe half smile.)

HONEY. Don't seem like snakes be good for nothin'.

SAVANNA. Hardly got 'nuff meat.

BULLET. Secret's how you fry 'em.

SINGING RAIN. She never fry snake.

ANAZET. Did you skin them first?

DINAH. Ain't never heard of fryin' no snakes.

BULLET. Ya git hungry 'nuff, you'd fry mud. Miracle you ain't.

SAVANNA. What's that word mean?

(The women listen as horses approach and become still. They listen to the dismounting and scattered foot steps. They collectively become fearful.)

*(Suddenly **CONCHATA** softly knocks on the door in signal.)*

*(**CONCHATA**'s single is non-verbal, "I Love you, Momma.")*

*(**SINGING RAIN** softly knocks in reply: "I Love you, Conchata.")*

HONEY. What ya say?

DINAH. I'm beside ya, I'm behind ya, alla 'round ya-

HONEY/DINAH. I'm wit ya.

*(**CONCHATA** knocks softly again, again **RAIN** responds.)*

*(The women remember **CONCHATA** and evolve into loving fierce warriors in response. Their posture changes along with attitude. Lights dim creating dark leaf pattern and darken deeper. Pause. In a sudden the shelter is hit with a barrage of bullets. Playwright strongly suggests this sequence be directed in slow motion, but do not drag scene out.)*

(There is screaming and shouting. **SINGING RAIN** *runs to the trap door, and as she does, she is the first to be killed. Then* **BULLET**. *The shelter becomes full of smoke/smoky light.* **HONEY** *is hit with bullets but does not die immediately. Only barely can it be seen that* **HONEY**, *then* **DINAH** *(a quick death) follow in death.)*

(The shelter is smoky. The door is thrown open. The bodies are scattered about. Boots, rifle tip and pants of a man (Jeremiah) are visible as he walks about the shelter with a lantern in hand examining the dead. He pauses at **ANAZET**, *kicks her over, prods her with rifle, and rests his boot on her chest, slightly pumping to make sure she is dead. Satisfied, finally, he spits then exits. There is rustling as the footsteps fade. Shadows, smoke and silence. After a moment, the sound: inaudible whispers.)*

(Slowly lights expressing night transition day. Pattern of morning sun and leaves. In the shadows **SAVANNA** *ever so slowly rises, then* **ANAZET**. *They help* **CONCHATA** *out of the trap door. It is the only hug in the play:* **SAVANNA** *and* **ANAZET** *hug* **CONCHATA**. *They check the dead.* **CONCHATA** *lies on the floor with her mother.* **ANAZET** *and* **SAVANNA** *cover the dead, ripping blankets to cover them and checking the outsides. Ever so often they stop and breathe, adjust their clothes, and basically try to gather themselves. They begin to pick up speed in leaving the shelter. Scene above is brief as lights come up, sound of all the living, birds, horses gently returns.)*

Scene Three

(Daybreak. Gun smoke-lighting clearing. Natural sounds return. The bodies of **BULLET, DINAH,** *and* **HONEY** *are half covered waist to face with torn blankets and cloth only slightly bloodied. All bodies, except* **SINGING RAIN** *are lying on the floor to the side of shack out of the way. Overturned furniture blocks bodies from audience especially from the waist up to neck/heads to avoid distraction.* **CONCHATA** *and* **SINGING RAIN** *are also to the side, downstage.)*

ANAZET. What about them?

(Pause. They look at the bodies.)

SAVANNA. Burn the shelter.

ANAZET. But the tree... She's still standing.

(They look up at the tree.)

SAVANNA. Yeah. *(softly acknowledging the tree and the truth)*

*(***CONCHATA** *is praying.* **SAVANNA** *and* **ANAZET** *pause looking at her.)*

CONCHATA. We give you our Love Creator for the new morning. Thank you. Thank you for my breath, for your sky, your sun, for brother sister birds, thank you. Thank you for mother Dinah, mother Honey, and mother Bullet, thank you for my mother...my mother...

*(***CONCHATA** *lays her mother gently down and cover her from waist to head.* **SINGING RAIN***'s face and body is turned upstage to avoid distraction.* **CONCHATA** *removes the remaining herbs/herb leaves, flowers/flower petals, and feathers from the pouches. Gently scattering and placing the herbs, flowers and feathers over all the bodies–generously covering her mother–ceremonially, but not slowly.)*

SAVANNA. Conchata, we gotta leave out.

ANAZET. *(over her shoulder as she continues gathering)* I'll be taking her.

SAVANNA. What?

CONCHATA. We go together.

ANAZET. *(Over her shoulder to* **SAVANNA.***)* I can only explain her.

SAVANNA. You ain't takin' her!

ANAZET. What have you to offer?

(**ANAZET** *begins to walk to* **CONCHATA.**)

SAVANNA. *(to* **CONCHATA***)* I'll give you everything I got.

ANAZET. You can't even give her a last name. Don't argue! I'm the better to make provisions. I will provide for this child, my child that I should have had. I've provided for myself. The riches I acquire will be hers too. *(to* **CONCHATA***)* We must leave!

(*As* **ANAZET** *rapidly approaches* **CONCHATA** *to gather her up,* **SAVANNA** *jumps* **ANAZET** *and pulls her gun.*)

SAVANNA. I'll kill you.

ANAZET. NO! Ahh!

CONCHATA. NO!

SAVANNA. They take my sisters, they take my body, and they rope me. Not my lil girl. Not my lil girl!

ANAZET.	**CONCHATA.**
Put it down…put it down…	Savanna, stop! Don't hurt her!

SAVANNA. You're not takin' her! Ya hear me?

ANAZET. I had my chance to leave, but I stayed. I wouldn't hurt her.

SAVANNA. But you might sell her!

ANAZET. Never!

SAVANNA. Say it!

ANAZET. I won't ever sell her.

SAVANNA. She won't never be whipped!

ANAZET. She won't!

SAVANNA. –Never be violated.

ANAZET. Please, let me go.

CONCHATA. *(struggles in vain to pull the two apart)* Please Savanna, please!

SAVANNA. What 'bout what Bullet wants...?

CONCHATA. They don't know...they don't know...

SAVANNA. Ya own momma, what 'bout her?

CONCHATA. You're my mother, too...all of you, please.

(The following speech is directed at the shelter itself.)

SAVANNA. Where!!! Alla who?! Where my sistas? Who my momma? I ain't nobodies nobody.

*(**SAVANNA** brings the gun down, dazed and hurting. **ANAZET** moves away.)*

CONCHATA. Savanna. You Love me. I know you Love me. I know you give me your life. But, my mother and my mother Bullet, they don't know. They don't know. I never say, but I hurt. They worry for food, they worry to hide me, they worry to run, but I hurt, my legs hurt. They want to grow but I live in earth box. I never say but I don't want sleep. I wait for my mother to sleep, to stop, to stop, stop! I'm afraid. If I stay awake she won't die. My mother holds me, I feel her heart always fast. I'm afraid. No more I hide. No caves, no horse cars, no earth box. I want sky. I want sun. Savanna, I want you bless me. If I alone, I have your bless, if I with horses, I have your bless, if they hang me-

SAVANNA. -THEY AIN'T GON' HANG YOU!!!

CONCHATA. Bless me, Savanna, I want to stand straight like you. I want my legs to stand straight. Bless me!

*(**SAVANNA** does not move. **CONCHATA** fiercely kisses **SAVANNA**'s forehead and holds her own to **SAVANNA** to kiss)*

CONCHATA. *(**CONCHATA** shakes **SAVANNA**)* Bless me! Bless me now! NOW!

*(**SAVANNA** looks at **CONCHATA** differently. She then kisses and blesses **CONCHATA**. They do not hug. This is not a mushy moment. Remain strong and survival clear. **ANAZET** runs to the door checking.)*

SAVANNA. *(to **CONCHATA**)* Somethin' go wrong, you come lookin' for me. You can't tell my face, remember this.

(SAVANNA unties her neck scarf to show CONCHATA the "hanging" scar. Before anyone can stop CONCHATA, she takes the knife from her leg, a la SAVANNA, and nicks her own throat. SAVANNA notices the cut and ties her own scarf around CONCHATA's neck. ANAZET and SAVANNA halt in shock, but quickly ANAZET continues moving fast.)

CONCHATA. Me too.

ANAZET. Say goodbye.

(SAVANNA and CONCHATA look at one another but they do not embrace.)

May I become your mother, too? *(silence)*

(Nearly defeated, SAVANNA looks away. ANAZET speaks softly, sensitive to SAVANNA.)

My new name is Ada Margaret Jordon…and your new name is–

CONCHATA. –Savanna. Conchata Singing Rain Bullet Savanna Honey Dinah.

(pause)

SAVANNA. Say it.

ANAZET. Conchata Singing Rain Bullet Savanna Honey Dinah.

SAVANNA. *(to ANAZET)* I'll come from the dead for her.

ANAZET. *(looks at the bodies)* I suspect that you all will. My promise stands.

SAVANNA. She best be all them riches you plannin' on gainin'.

(ANAZET removes the only ring from her finger.)

ANAZET. Here, take this, my triumph.

SAVANNA. Ya tryin' to buy me?

ANAZET. Slavers can be bought, hunters bartered with. I know.

SAVANNA. You killed him, ain't ya?

ANAZET. Why? Because I didn't stop her. *(not a question)*

SAVANNA. Ya–

ANAZET. –I will not be put down. *(slighly softer, no less potent)* Will you?

> *(SAVANNA, a little dazed, turns her back. CONCHATA, remembering Dinah, walks to the jar/vase holding the flower that is still standing through the chaos. She retrieves Dinah's wildflower. ANAZET, determindley but sensitive to SAVANNA, gathers up her last things. CONCHATA and ANAZET move at the same time, maintianing tension/urgency.)*

> *(SAVANNA doesn't look at them.)*

SAVANNA. Take MyZion.

CONCHATA. You Love him.

SAVANNA. *(to CONCHATA)* Remember us.

> *(Although SAVANNA's back is to ANAZET, she extends her hand.)*

ANAZET. Savanna. You make it, hear?

> *(ANAZET gently touches SAVANNA's arm. In reflex, SAVANNA turns around with her arm lifted. Quickly, ANAZET shakes her hand.)*

ANAZET. Good Luck!

> *(Quickly she bends down, lifts saddle, rushes CONCHATA to door. SAVANNA stands in a a sad daze.)*

ANAZET. *(at the door to SAVANNA, trying to shake her)* GIT OUTTA HERE GAL!

CONCHATA. Spirit will help Savanna!

> *(ANAZET holding CONCHATA's hand she halts at the door, takes a very deep breath, they exit rushing. Sound: horse riding off and fading. Slowly, SAVANNA overturns her palm, ANAZET's ring drops to the floor.)*

> *(SAVANNA quickly chases about the shelter collecting the remains of guns, straightening out the blankets covering the dead. She covers SINGING RAIN's head and stops in mid-motion.*

(She stands dazed. Lost with the realization that she is again alone. She walks to the shack door and is suddenly seized with fear. She goes to the windows and takes aim. She runs in all directions with her guns aimed at anything, everything. She relives the thought of the train car attack. Lost, she collapses in a corner. Softly, barely audible classical music begins playing and continues behind the following speech. Slowly, she drops her guns, overwhelmed with fear. Lights slowly dim. She crawls to and then stands up in the center of the shack. Lights continue to dim as she stands. She speaks with a heavy rasp.)

(Suggested music: Samuel Barber: Agnus Dei Adagio for strings plays underneath the following speech.)

SAVANNA. Here I am. Can you see even me? Come. Here I am. I was the one–when they spooked that horse. Come Spirit, come get me I'm on the tree. Come take me from the tree, please…I ain't never been down from the tree. Come Spirit take me off the tree…my name's Savanna, that's all I'm wearin'.

(Pause. Slow and unsteady **SAVANNA** *goes to her knees.)*

Take me…Take me too, Spirit. *(She is trying to pray.)* Thank you for my breath…thank you for the sky…for my sista Dinah, my sista, Honey, come Spirit, for Miss Bullet…for Rain…watch over Anazet and my child, Conchata. Come good and mighty Spirit watch over me too. Watch over me too. I your child too. I your child too, I too… *(A feeling has changed.)* Thank you. Thank you, thank you.

*(**SAVANNA** slowly hugs herself and ever so gentle the lights brighten into new day.)*

I'm gon' be all right? I'm gon' be all right. I'm gon' be all right…right. Thank you.

*(**SAVANNA**'s voice begins cracking. The raspy sound fades. Smoke {smoky lighting} has cleared. By the end of her speech her voice is free and clear. For the first time some*

branches on tree ever so slightly sway. Subtlety is key. She hears **MYZION** *snorting and realizes they have left him for her. Quickly she gathers her saddle bag, picks up the little bird made of branches. She puts the ring in saddle bag, lifts the bird high over her head as they begin to exit. She halts at the door. She takes one last look at the bodies.* **MYZION** *whinnies louder and she lifts the little bird and they both exit flying.)*

(Offstage she triumphantly calls:)

SAVANNA. MyZion!

MYZION. *(whinnies. translation: "Yeah, it's me!")*

(She flies the bird and exits.)

(The sound of a single horse galloping off and fading. Tree sways.)

(Suggested music: Schubert: Ave Maria/Opera or Enya: Fairytale plays softly, gently under the following dialogue to end.)

(As opening scene: seven spirit women stand in dark silhouette in semi-circle. They are in various prayer levels and positions. **SINGING RAIN** *is in the center. The women are whispering their prayers. Their eyes remain closed to the end of play. Faint sound of* **MYZION** *whinnies.)*

(Enter **ADULT CONCHATA** *as very prosperous wealthy woman.)*

*(***ADULT CONCHATA** *is poised, powerful. Regal as she speaks directly to the audience. She pauses and then begins.)*

ADULT CONCHATA. Once, long ago when I had small soft legs, I lived in the midst of the woods, under the blue pines, near the rivers. I had seven mothers, seven wonder filled mothers when I lived in the midst of the woods, who gave me who I am.

(pause)

*(Enter **CHARLOTTE**.)*

(A little girl appears angel-like in gauze white gown, barefoot.)

CHARLOTTE. *(softly calling)*	**HONEY.** *(eyes closed)*
Here I am…Here I am… Here I am…	Charlotte

*(**CHARLOTTE** comes from audience (if possible) stands between **HONEY** and **DINAH**. **CHARLOTTE** takes their hands and looks up grazing at **HONEY**, smiling. She continues smiling at her mother as the lights fade to black.)*

THE END

THREADS

Fairytale-culture-style: Energy, audacity, spirit independent. Emotional clothes. Beautiful fairytale threads shifted by wind, tree branches, tattered by midnight stars, unraveling grit. The women as trampled fruit, styled by rushing wind…but beautiful like the women, all natural materials. One get-up (costume) per character. Threads accommodate horse riding and hidden weapons.

SAVANNA, HONEY, DINAH, ADULT CONCHATA dress in the purple/collard green family. **BULLET, SINGING RAIN, CONCHATA** in forest green/suede family. **ANAZET** in white and black/dark.

SAVANNA

Scarf styled around neck. Female-fitted (somewhat) shirt. Pants: fitted suede or work material, not a patch in sight. Worn riding boots. Generous brim hat. Stylish waist coat optional. Hair: Off the face. Perhaps low pony tail or stylishly short. It's about with the horse. Worn clothes never sloppy.

ANAZET

Fitted tailored white blouse, pearl buttons. Dark flared skirt, fitted waist. Lady-like riding boots. Two shiny gold rings. Pearl earrings. Hair: Off face, wavy. Option: elegant sparkling hair pins…she's got it like that. Finest of "I love myself" materials.

BULLET

Herb pouch worn around neck. Queen out of context. Empire dress. A blend among the curvaceous trees. Strong not sexless. Work Boots. Option: Yoruba beads around neck, some tucked in dress. Hair: Wrapped material queen-style, as if a crown. Option: Dreads or braids wrapped crown-like high enough to hide a knife.

SINGING RAIN

Herb pouch worn around neck. One shouldered, mid-calf dress made with textured material. A slash across the body. May add feathers (do not overdo it) or the idea of flight. Soft color–not faint. No fringe. No beads. Dress has an un-raveling effect. Worn boots. Hair: Partially twisted off face, loose, expressing emotional interior.

CONCHATA

Herb pouch worn around neck. Simple dress created with fragile cloth, as if a bird weaved it…especially the back (where she lays beneath the trap-door, slightly tattered by earth). May appear as if she has out grown it. Shoes: Bootie-style. Suede cloth wrapped around feet, tie with leather strips, they do not fall off. Hair: Styled by the forest. Twig or vine twisted in it, a hidden flower-free, but not sloppy. The women do do her hair.

CHARLOTTE
Everything but the wings. Dress of gauzy, tulle, cotton white, creams or yellow to the knee. Lovely float of faint color, a cloud dressed her. Barefoot berry stained toes. Spirit Ghost. Hair: Soft-tender. Maybe a blond 'fro or 'fro of waves. Not Easter Sunday.

HONEY
Voluptuous. Trampled fruit in a dress. Consider: romantic plum, berry. Fitted through the waist, flares slightly, (earth/floor length) long. Boots. Hair: Huge hair, nearly a 'fro or giant ocean waves and curls.

DINAH
Sassy-sweet. Consider: plum, magenta and unleashed heat. Fitted through the waist, flairs, (floor/earth length) long. Attire somewhat a little bloody. Boots. HAIR: Younger sister giant. Unbound.

ADULT CONCHATA (In her late 20s)
Wealthy, exquisite, stylish refined combo of culture and currency. Long dress, fitted at waist. Finest material. Consider: Amethyst elegant. Rich Riding boots. Gold rings. **ANAZET** who kept her promise, she better!

MAN IN BOOTS
Visible from pants/knees down only. Soiled work pants. Dirty muddy heavy big boots. Menace.

Women and child wear gold hoop earrings (no studs) except **ANAZET** who wears pearls. All women have plum/berry stained lips. All women and children have berry stained nails.

THE FEMALE TREE
Voluptuous thick slightly curvy trunk. Large sweeping branches loaded with leaves. Lush dark green, shimmers, spiritual, medicinal not for tasting. It is its own creation. Does it flower? Give fruit? Didn't say. If she sang it would be Aretha, Mahalia or Dinah W.'s pipes...someday all three. Sometimes just Patty L.

MYZION (Heard but not seen...but you can negotiate)
The man. Large, black, white blurry star in forehead. Strong, elegant and most intelligent. What would they do without him? He knows it.

JUDAH (Heard but not seen/just the way he likes it.)
Brown and white. Smaller. Educated by Myzion. Polite. Doesn't confuse matters. Said, that's all you need to know.

ALL THE LIVING
Morning sun. Night wind. Stars. Moon. River. Mountain. Birds and, all of God's creatures. Spirit. Earth Forest...Welcome Wildlife!

Love.

BELONGINGS

Saddles
Rifles
Hand guns
Knives

Candles/lantern
Old yellowing papers with hand drawn portrait: Wanted: Bullet
Large carved wooden bowl with ladle
Bundles of forest herbs, flowers, leaves & such

Gold rings (**ANAZET**)

Bird of branches (**CONCHATA**)

Wooden bracelet (**SAVANNA**)

Pearl buttons (**ANAZET**)

Gold hoop earrings (**HONEY, DINAH, SAVANNA, BULLET, CONCHATA, SINGING RAIN**)

Suede Neck herb pouches (**BULLET, SINGING RAIN, CONCHATA**)

Love.

SET

A fairy-tale shelter with a strong majestic feminine tree with curves growing in the mist of it. One branch holds a child's tiny swing. It is only seen when it is pulled down-otherwise it is tucked up into the tree. A child-size hidden door dug into the earth floor in front of the tree, as if it is a part of the tree. It is only big enough for a child to lay down, cramped. A rug made of material and vines disguises and covers the trap door. Two beautifully carved fairy tale beds created with bark, vines, and leaves. Matching fairy tale table and chairs. Two carved stools. Two windows. A door double bolted with tree limbs. A rack of sticks holding suede pouches of herbs, flowers, fruits, nuts. The shelter is neat, clear, minimalism but not empty. However, brief, evident it is women who dwell here.

One huge majestic tree, shiny leaves, not flowering with
A child's tiny swing: swing seat made of suede/skins or natural material
Two Fairytale beds; small slim created with branches & forest material, fairytale bedding, not regular size
Wood vine twisted Table, somewhat chairs and stool/wood stump
Craved stool and matching side table

Branches holding hanging herbs, flowers, fruits and nuts
Woven rug of cloth, vines, feathers and forest material
Dinner plates; large leaves, wooden bowl or slices of clean tree-plate
Bags/Pouches: fruit; nuts; berries
Bucket
Blanket like materials
Love.

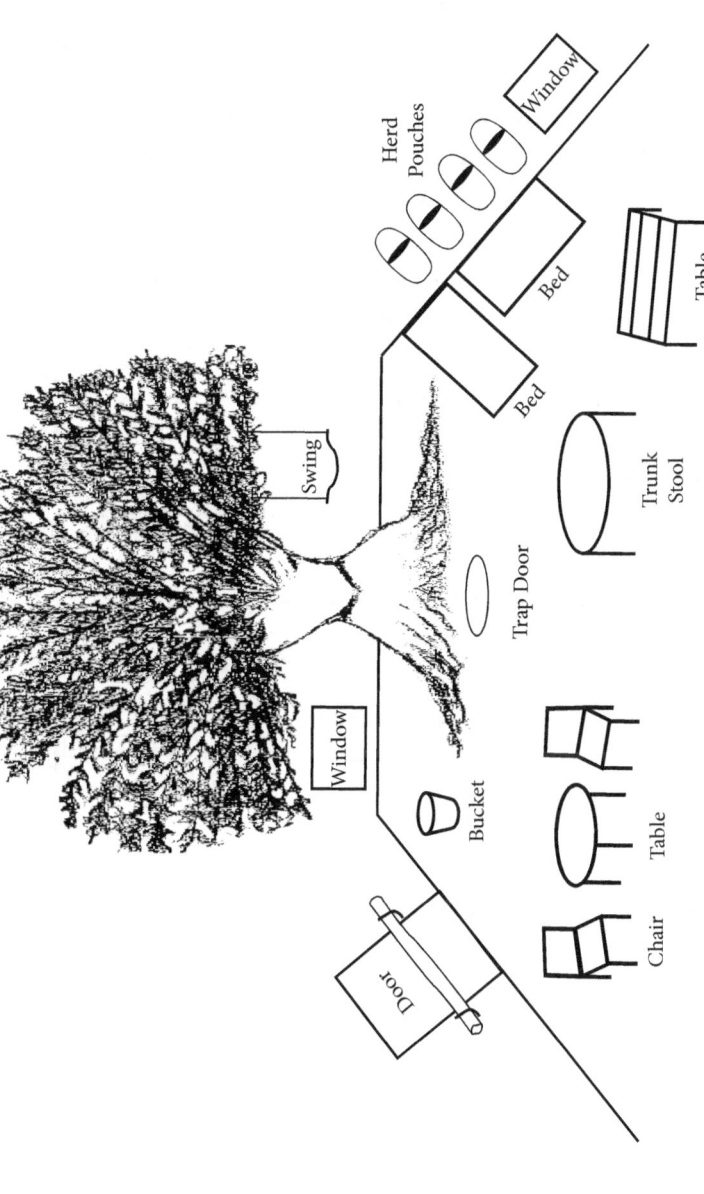

Wildlife! set design by Ramona King

See what people are saying about
WILDLIFE!...

"Extremely compelling! Seven strong women with wonderful messageswas more than compelling – it was an epiphany!"

"The play was so spiritual…connecting people, nature, horses."

"Elegance, humor, originality"

"Glad that you took in a story of our Holocaust. We need these stories told and by us!"

"The writing was beautiful, powerful, amazing character."

"Your talent is scary."

"This is a unique story that needs telling. I loved it!"

"The emotion was almost a physical force."

"Everyone is talking about it – not getting out of their seats."

"Absolutely wonderful."

OTHER TITLES AVAILABLE FROM SAMUEL FRENCH

ALL THROUGH THE NIGHT

Shirley Lauro

Drama / 5f / Simple Set

Nominee! 2006 Joseph Jefferson nomination as Best New Chicago Play of the Year

All Through the Night speaks directly with a warning for today. Set during and after the Third Reich, a stylistic, surrealistic play inspired by interviews with German Gentile women. The play sweeps from their teen years through adulthood during the Holocaust and beyond. The Nazi Regime impacts the women's lives as they struggle over work, religion, marriage and motherhood. Making overwhelmingly hard choices, they survive or succumb to Hitler's Reign and are changed forever.

A sylistic, surrealistic play. Minimal set and minimal props. An unconventional timeframe that jumps a chronological order

"Events...elevated to artistic dramatization. Most interesting is character transformations as the stories unfold."
– *Backstage*

"Intensely moving...a compelling play...smart yet strikingly sympathetic...significant!"
– Chris Jones, *Chicago Tribune*

"No story less told than what happened to the German Christian women (in WWII)...such relevance to what is happening now...fascinating...the emotional side of war …"
– *Time Out*

"A gem. Highly recommended. Remarkable. One of the finest new works shown on a Chicago stage in several years...seldom have I seen such a polished, smartly constructed work! Rich in drama and emotion...wonderfully written...SEE THIS SHOW!"
– *ChicagoCritic.com*

SAMUELFRENCH.COM

OTHER TITLES AVAILABLE FROM SAMUEL FRENCH

BULRUSHER

Eisa Davis

Drama / 3m, 3f

Finalist for the 2007 Pulitzer Prize in Drama

In 1955, in the redwood country north of San Francisco, a multiracial girl grows up in a predominantly white town whose residents pepper their speech with the historical dialect of Boontling. Found floating in a basket on the river as an infant, Bulrusher is an orphan with a gift for clairvoyance that makes her feel like a stranger even amongst the strange: the taciturn schoolteacher who adopted her, the madam who runs her brothel with a fierce discipline, the logger with a zest for horses and women, and the guitar-slinging boy who is after Bulrusher's heart. Just when she thought her world might close in on her, she discovers an entirely new sense of self when a black girl from Alabama comes to town. Passionate, lyrical, and chock full of down-home humor, this play is an unforgettable experience by a new, thrilling voice.

"[Davis] tickles the ears of her listeners…moving scenes on the banks of the pebble-strewn river…feel utterly true."
– *The New York Times*

"Davis explores her themes in unexpected and evocative ways ….The still waters of Bulrusher turn out to run pretty deep."
– *The San Francisco Chronicle*

"…an engrossing rush…Eisa Davis' gleaming marriage of poetry and myth… has a big heart and a wide-open soul."
– *Minneapolis-St. Paul Star Tribune*

SAMUELFRENCH.COM

OTHER TITLES AVAILABLE FROM SAMUEL FRENCH

NEST

Bathsheba Doran

Drama / 5m, 2f

Based on historical fact, *Nest* is a taut domestic love triangle set against the landscape of a fledgling nation on the verge of realizing its manifest destiny at a terrible bloody cost. The play re-imagines the real life story of Susanna Cox, a young indentured servant from Pennsylvania who murdered her baby in 1809, and the story of the man who wrote the ballad that was sold at her hanging. The play is a searing exploration of American dreams and violence and their place in the national psyche.

"[Susanna Cox's] tale is uniquely American, involving all our national obsessions: sexuality, class, gender roles, the search for national identity, and, most of all, the insidious, hypocritical piety coded into our cultural DNA...Doran is particularly deft at constructing dialogue filled with small, characterizing moments to elucidate her themes."
– *Washington City Paper*

"Bathsheba Doran has crafted this seemingly simple but gripping 90-minute work from the true story of Susanna Cox"
– *TalkinBroadway.com*

"Nest...is no simple costume-drama rendering of [a] young woman's life and death....When the artificial walls of the earlier scenes fall away and the stage is flooded by the cast working as a kind of chorus, one feels the heart of the playwright."
– *MetroWeekly*

SAMUELFRENCH.COM

www.ingramcontent.com/pod-product-compliance
Lightning Source LLC
Chambersburg PA
CBHW070648300426
44111CB00013B/2326